Don't Play The Woman Card

The Intense Queens of Heart

By
Katrina Eddy

Copyright © 2025 by Katrina Eddy

All Rights Reserved. No part of this publication may be reproduced, stored in a retrieval system, or transmitted, in any form or by any means, electronic, mechanical, photocopying, recording, or otherwise, without the written permission of the author.

Published by: USA Publishing Hub
www.USApublishinghub.com

This book is dedicated to:

My brother Matt – You have been my inspiration my entire life, even after you passed away. I love you forever and a day.

February 1977 – May 2015

***

To my family and friends,

I'm sorry I never shared some of these things with you. Please know that I'm okay now—I'm working through my past traumas and healing. I've made peace with what happened and am moving forward. I've removed the toxic souls I kept in my life for too long, both friends and family, and I'm healing—mind, body, and soul. It's a slow process, but it's moving forward. I love you all, and thank you for standing by me.

—Katrina

For those who never felt heard.

For those who never felt seen.

For the outcasts in the family.

For those who speak their mind, only to be silenced.

Welcome—you are part of the family now.

***

This book is written in Arial font to help my friends and family with dyslexia read it more easily. I love you all—enjoy. <3

Contents

Prelude 1

Chapter 1	Background / Growing Up 6
Chapter 2	High School 16
Chapter 3	College 46
Chapter 4	Abuse 53
Chapter 5	Drugs and Drinking 66
Chapter 6	Working 74
Chapter 7	"Why Do You ____ Like That?" 86
Chapter 8	Finding Yourself 91
Chapter 9	Becoming A "Bonus Parent" 105
Chapter 10	Losing a Loved One 105
Chapter 11	Raising A Strong Girl 116
Chapter 12	Now As a Business Owner 119
Chapter 13	Career Change in Your Thirties 127
Chapter 14	Marriage and Having a Partner 133
Chapter 15	Writing A Book 136

Prelude

If you don't understand what a woman fights for, you'll never understand that woman—or any woman, for that matter. Women are expected to work like we don't have kids and parent like we don't work. We can't get sick. If we take a break or have an off day, everyone loses their minds, and the household falls apart.

Men and women are built differently, and that's what makes us great. I could never lift as much as my husband, and I will never be as physically strong as him. On the other hand, he will never be as mentally strong as I am. That's not to say there aren't physically strong women and mentally strong men, but statistically, this is reality. And here's the thing—**that's okay!**

Men complement women, and women complement men. But in today's world, women are expected to act, dress, and parent a certain way, and I believe we are losing our voices—losing what makes us great.

I'm not a Republican or a Democrat. I'm not Christian or otherwise. I am a free thinker. I try my best to see all points of view. I have my own beliefs, opinions, and reasons for saying what I do. The thing is, I've lived through a lot, and I survived it all. And so can you.

Before I dive into the rest of the prelude—and then the book—I want to make something clear. Yes, this book is mainly directed toward women, but that doesn't mean it's not for men too. It's for anyone who needs to know they're not alone.

When I was drafting this book, I spoke with several photographers for the cover and some of the pictures you'll see throughout. Since you're reading this, you've obviously seen the cover—I'm burning the queen card. That symbolizes destroying female stereotypes, stepping over the "get in the kitchen and make me a sandwich" mentality (not that I can cook anyway, haha). It rejects the idea that women are dumber than men, that we're just objects, that our worth is only in our looks or what's between our legs.

One photographer told me I should burn the king card instead because "men in general are scum and a waste of oxygen." But that's not true. Are there horrible men in the world? Absolutely. But there are horrible women too. I have no interest in pushing a fake agenda. I love my husband, my father, my son, my stepson, my brothers, and my brothers-in-law.

Most men understand a woman's worth. But as my mom once told an ex of mine: "You can do a million good things, but it's the one bad thing people will remember." And I believe that's true. We see terrible men all over social media and the news, and yes, they are horrible people. But we can't label all men based on what a few idiots do. Most men take care of their women—but plenty don't.

I want to break the stereotype that "all men are bad" because they aren't. That's one of my goals with this book—along with showing men and women alike that they're not alone in what they feel, what they've gone through, and how they think. I also hope it gives men some insight into what women typically experience.

My name is Katrina. I'm a mother, a stepmother, a wife, a former business owner, and an advocate for many things. I speak my mind. Life has made my skin thick, but I'm ready to use my past pain for something good—to help others.

The goal of my book is to empower women (and men) to be exactly who they are meant to be. Whether you're a stay-at-home parent, a business owner, a housewife, an employee—whatever path you're on—you deserve to have your voice and advocate for yourself in every part of life.

I'm thirty-six. I don't claim to know everything, but I've lived through enough to help others find their strength.

I hope this book reaches the right people—the ones trying to find themselves again. Maybe you're a nervous new mom, someone getting sober, or a person who just quit their job. Maybe you're feeling lost after a divorce or a major life change. Maybe you're a woman trying to enter a male-dominated field and need guidance. Maybe you're struggling to figure out how to speak in today's world, where everyone takes offense to everything.

I see a need to show a different side of womanhood and chasing dreams. I want women—people—who read this book to know that I've been where you are. I've had the same doubts, fears, and insecurities. And we are moving forward anyway.

I'll leave you with a quote that sums up exactly how I feel:

Don't Play the Woman Card

Three things I do not like when people talk to me:

Do not talk to me like I am a child.

Do not talk to me like I am supposed to fear you.

Do not talk to me like I am stupid.

Chapter 1

Background / Growing Up

I grew up in Massachusetts, in a small town outside of Boston. I was raised in a loving home with both parents and had two brothers. I had friends, got good grades, and was your typical "tomboy." I played in the dirt and mud, was the quarterback for the Saugus Police League football team, and played video games. I feel like my upbringing really shaped me and helped me think the way I do.

Here is my first point: When I was growing up, I was a typical "tomboy," and today, it seems like that is almost looked down upon. My oldest niece was the same as me. She was more comfortable in baggy pants than fitted ones, didn't wear makeup, wanted to play contact sports, was opinionated, and most importantly, she was strong. She was picked on for how she dressed, for her ponytail, and for having opinions. She was told no one would want to date her because of that, and she was only a pre-teen. After being constantly picked on, she changed herself to fit the "norm." She wore fitted clothes, low-cut shirts, covered her face in makeup, and lost her voice. Why are we putting out the fires in these girls' souls? They will need those fires to advocate for themselves someday.

My message to young girls is this: Do not worry about what other people think of you. I made that mistake, and I regret it. Just be the best version of yourself. You NEVER have to put a label on who you are unless you want to. Do not let others define you, and certainly do not ever lose your voice to people who do not matter in the end.

I attended preschool through middle school in my hometown of Saugus, Massachusetts. It was a quiet town where most people knew each other. My father owned a small business; he was the "floor guy," and everyone knew him. One of the highlights of my childhood was working for my dad. I felt strong and empowered, and I loved spending time with him. He taught me many life lessons that I still use today. I know that when my dad reads this, he will roll his eyes just like I did every time he tried to teach me something, but as much as I rolled my eyes, everything stuck. My dad was my hero growing up, and he still is, even though I am now 36 years old. Much of how my dad raised me influences how I raise my children. I try to instill the same morals in them that he instilled in my brothers and me. The most important lesson he taught me was to have a voice and to be myself. I was an independent, opinionated kid, and my dad knew how to keep me grounded while also allowing me to think for myself. I cannot thank him enough for that.

I always had good grades, perfect attendance, and friends. I was your typical down-home, all-American girl. I was in Girl Scouts, played soccer, football, and softball, had a pony growing up, and spent my childhood in the saddle. I got my first "real job" as soon as I could at age twelve. I worked for my dad for years and learned a strong work ethic from him. I also learned that I wanted a marriage like my parents had. My mom was the brains behind my dad's company, and my dad was the "horse." Though my parents' marriage didn't last, they gave me something to strive for. They showed me the importance of being a partner—whether in marriage, friendship, or family.

Elementary school was difficult for me. I was diagnosed with epilepsy in 1996, just before I turned seven. I had about 200 seizures a day, which made me a target for bullying. In third grade, a boy in my class told me, "You know you can die, right?" This devastated me. I understood what death was, and it terrified me. When I was diagnosed, the school wanted to fast-track me into special education classes, but at seven years old, I already had the mindset of "Test me, and I will prove you wrong." And I did. I stayed in regular classes and moved into AP classes as soon as they became available.

So here's my next lesson for young girls AND boys: Don't let someone define you—fight like hell. Some kids and adults need extra help, and there is nothing wrong with that. But in my case, I knew I didn't need the school system deciding how I should learn.

My husband, for instance, has severe dyslexia, but he is one of the smartest people I know. He is quick with math, an amazing mason, and remembers every detail about job sites. Another example is my brother Matt, who passed away in 2015. He had muscular dystrophy, but he was one of the smartest people I knew. Then there's my niece, the one I mentioned earlier. She is on the spectrum, but she can solve college-level math problems at age twelve and is an incredible artist.

The point is this: No matter your age or disability, find your voice, find what sets your soul on fire, and do it. Don't let someone else tell you how smart or talented you are or how you should learn. Every person is their own bit of awesomeness, and that should be celebrated.

I continued to play sports, and my teachers started recognizing my intelligence. One of them told my parents, "Her brain is like a sponge—she retains EVERYTHING." Looking back, I am so glad I didn't listen to the school board, and I am so grateful my parents advocated for me—especially my mom. She was incredibly involved in my education, health, and life in general. As a kid, it was annoying, but now that I'm older and have my own kids, I understand. If I had given in and done what the school said, I would have limited my abilities and never known what I was capable of.

In 2000, I moved up to middle school and was excited, but it became a whole new challenge. New teachers. More kids. My town had five elementary schools but only one middle school. After proving myself in elementary school, I had to start all over again.

I entered middle school in September 2000 for sixth grade. I was thrilled to be with older kids and my cousins, who had gone to different elementary schools. I did well, but my epilepsy started causing problems again, leading to more bullying. Now I was the "weird kid" who had to leave class to take medication. I was called "crazy," "retarded," "stupid," and more. People constantly asked what was wrong with me. I had to miss school dances because flashing lights triggered my seizures. All of this led to relentless bullying.

Depression hit me hard, even though I was young. I finally convinced my parents to let me attend a dance in seventh grade. They weren't thrilled, knowing the lights would trigger seizures. But when I arrived, I was surprised—one of my friends had spoken to the DJ, who adjusted the lighting. The dance floor was split so I could safely enjoy myself. That night was incredible.

Growing up, many girls my age talked about boys, crushes, and first kisses. I had none of that, and it made me feel different. Overcoming bullying for my epilepsy was one thing, but now I was bullied for not being interested in boys. I was called "gay" because I hadn't had my first kiss. But after that dance, I realized growing up is about finding lifelong friends, not just a partner. To this day, I still have friends from middle school.

Eventually, I did have my first kiss and my first boyfriend in seventh grade. It didn't last, but I kept pushing myself to get out and make new friends.

One day I will never forget is September 11, 2001. I was in biology class when the TV turned on. We saw smoke billowing from skyscrapers in New York, and then another plane hit. Our teacher quickly shut the TV off. Twenty minutes later, a friend was called to the office, and we didn't see her again that day.

When I got home, my mom sat me down. I don't remember the whole conversation, but she told me bad things were happening in the world and that our military would protect us. My grandfather, a proud Marine, always said, "You don't need to love your government, but you do need to love your neighbor." That day, I decided I would enlist as a Marine when I turned 18.

I wrote a term paper in seventh grade about where we saw ourselves in ten years. What career did we want to have? Did we want to have kids? (Because it was okay to ask this back then.) Or did we want to further our education? I remember reading it aloud to the class. I had brought in all these different things my grandfather gave me—dog tags, pictures, books, etc. I talked about how I loved my country and how my grandfather was a Marine. And now, because of what happened with the terrorists, I wanted to go overseas and fight to protect my country. I had no plans to have children, no plans to further my education—I just wanted to protect and serve my country.

After my presentation, someone chimed in and said, "Girls can't join the Marines. They are not strong enough." This set me off. I had just done all these things to prove I was strong, and now I was being told I wasn't strong enough. Granted, my teacher spoke up and told the boy that girls could do anything boys could do, but it still hurt. Little 12-year-old me didn't know what I was really going to do with my life or how strong and resilient I would end up being.

I rode out seventh grade and kept the "I want to be a Marine" to a minimum after that presentation. I feel like this was when I started to lose my voice a little and when I started caring more about what people thought and said about me. It was different in elementary school—the kids were younger, and there was less pressure to "be cool." I got good grades, held high honors, had perfect attendance, and was Student of the Month for four to five months. I was so proud of myself. I was still the weird kid for having to leave the classroom to take medicine, but the bullying from that slowed down. The new reason I was a target was my good grades and getting "Student of the Month." I was called a "teacher's pet" and a "kiss-ass." I ignored it because I knew how far I had come from having the school board tell me I needed to be in Special Education.

I entered eighth grade, which meant both of my cousins—who had been at middle school with me, protecting and standing up for me when needed—had now graduated and moved on to high school. Eighth grade started off well. I stayed in honors classes, held onto my honors and perfect attendance. By then, I was starting to like school. I had gone to more events over the summer, met more people, and was invited to more things. I was still almost losing my voice, just doing what people thought was cool. But I lost it enough that I became the bully I had hated so much for years—all because the "cool" girls and boys in my classes told me to. I became not a nice person to some of my peers. I became the person I had once asked my friends and cousins to protect me from.

Girls are taught this behavior. I know most people have seen the movie *Mean Girls*, where the mom enables her daughter to have certain bad behaviors—trying to be the "cool mom." I saw this firsthand at a birthday party for one of these "cool girls." Her mom, while we were in eighth grade, was talking about things no parent should be discussing with kids, let alone someone else's kids. I heard these parents gossiping with their daughters about how to steal someone's boyfriend. They were "getting the tea," as we say today, meaning getting the gossip. To hear a parent say, "Wow, yeah, that girl is ugly," or "I see why you make fun of her," was absolutely appalling. At that moment, I realized being a "cool girl" wasn't worth it anymore.

I began to separate myself from these girls. I ignored them when I got to school and when I left. Finally, one girl asked me what my problem was. I told her I didn't like how she treated people and that I didn't like when she made fun of me either. She said, "You were acting just like us, and you had no problem with it." And right then, I realized—I *did* lose my voice. I had allowed these girls to control what I said and how I behaved, and I was ashamed of myself. I was better than this. But as a twelve- or thirteen-year-old, I was more interested in being included.

Looking back now, I am so upset with how easily I lost who I was.

Aside from wanting to be a Marine, I also wanted to be a vet. My goal was to serve on the front lines and later take care of K9 soldiers. I know when 9/11 happened, I swore I wouldn't further my education—I was all about just going to the front lines. But as I got older, things changed. That's when I decided I needed a fresh start. I wanted to go somewhere new for high school, where no one knew anything about me. I contacted the school I was interested in, set up a private interview, and only told my close friends that I would not be going to Saugus High with them.

Chapter 2

High School

I was listening to one of Steve Harvey's interviews, and I really liked what he said, so I'd like to share it:

"I saw a woman once, talking to a young girl. She said, 'Don't get in the habit of collecting red flags.' And she was right. She was a young girl—she shouldn't be collecting red flags. You start collecting red flags at a young age, you'll have a wagon full by the time you're eighteen years old."

Another great interview I heard I wish I could remember the woman's name because she was amazing—said something that stuck with me:

"You need to think about what legacy you are leaving behind. It's not all about you. Everything you do affects the people around you, whether you know them or not. It could be as simple as the way you say 'hello'—it may turn someone's day around. Or it could be the way you didn't hold the elevator for someone—you could send that person into a downward spiral. We never know what another person is going through. In this world, just be nice!"

I got into the school I wanted—Essex Agricultural and Technical High School, a well-known technical and agricultural school with a great vet program. I started at the end of August 2003. I was so excited—I could start fresh and be the person I wanted to be. I was the only one from my town who went to this new school, so no one knew who I was. Not that I would lie about who I was—that's not right—but I could put my poor behavior behind me, forget about those so-called "friends," and make the rest of my school career what I wanted it to be. I was excited to get my life moving.

I instantly loved the school. I met great people right away—some of whom I'm still friends with today. My freshman year, I was still set on being a vet, but we had to take all the majors—Plant Science, Animal Science, and Environmental Science—so we could try everything before choosing a direction for our senior year. I enjoyed every class I took and was doing well in all of them. I wasn't the "weird kid" anymore. I was on a 180-acre high school campus with a farm, and I finally felt like I had met good people. Life seemed to be turning around for the better.

About a month or so into my freshman year, I got a call from one of my close friends from my hometown, and boy, did he have some news for me. When I answered, we chatted for a while since we hadn't really seen each other much since I switched schools. My new school accepted students within a twenty-mile radius, so I didn't get home until much later. Luckily, things were going great for him, and he liked our town's high school. After catching up, our conversation went like this:

Him: "So, you're not going to believe what I heard today."

Me: "What's going on? Is everyone okay?"

Him: "Yeah, I heard you died."

AWKWARD SILENCE

Me: "I what?"

Him: "Yeah, I heard you died. Ha ha ha."

Me: "Oh, cool. When are my services? Ha ha ha."

Him: "Yeah, that's the big rumor since you didn't show up on the first day. I tried to tell people you went to a different school, but I think people still like to talk shit."

Me: "Who started it? Do you know?"

Then he told me. It was the girl I told off before leaving middle school and fully deciding to transfer.

Take this as a lesson—no matter what you do to better yourself, there will always be someone trying to put you down. If a person is constantly putting you down, they're not worth your stress. Over the years, I've learned that people—especially girls—can be incredibly mean to one another. Even when I wasn't a nice person, I never understood how people could be cruel enough to try to ruin someone's life or push them into depression just for entertainment or to feel better about their own insecurities.

As I got older, I realized you can't make everyone happy. I spent a good chunk of middle school being a "yes girl" and losing my voice to people who didn't matter—people who didn't bring me joy or positivity. I dwelled on it for a while, and in a way, my depression started creeping back. Even at my new school, I felt like I couldn't escape the mean girls from my town.

One morning, I woke up to messages and MySpace posts saying, "R.I.P." and "Gone too soon." My MySpace was blowing up. My new friends from school were seeing these posts. I immediately started deleting them, but I felt cornered. I've never handled feeling cornered well—it makes me feel like there's no way out.

Like any teenager, I didn't handle this well. I started cutting my ankles to take the pain away from my mind and send it to my body. I scratched my hands raw. I pinched my legs so hard I made myself bleed. I started skipping school, pretending to be sick. I was home more than I was at school. I still made sure my schoolwork was done, but I just didn't want to go.

It got so bad that I asked my parents if I could drop out. That conversation, big surprise, didn't go well. My parents asked, "Why would you want to drop out? You have all new friends, and you're getting good grades." I told them, "Well, Dad didn't graduate high school, and he's very successful. If he didn't finish high school, why do I have to?"

Looking back, I realize how unfair that was to say about my father. He's one of the smartest and most successful people I know. Eventually, I went back to school and faced my demons.

Growing up, I was—and still am—remarkably close with my dad. We bonded through music. I watched him play drums in bands when I was little. Music always spoke to me—the beats of every song became motivation. I truly believe the saying, "Pay attention to what a woman listens to—it'll tell you more than her words ever will."

I got into competitive dance and joined a studio in the next town over. I enjoyed it. It was a way to get my emotions out. A lot of what I heard growing up was, "It's okay, just put on a smile," or "Get over it," or "You're fine, just find something to do." I never really learned how to deal with depression or anxiety—I just pushed it down.

But when I started dancing, I became more confident. I remember my dance coach asking me, "Do you realize how pretty you are?" I said, "No. I feel like I'm constantly changing. I don't really know who I am. I *look* better, but I don't *feel* better. I'm just going through a lot."

I knew I needed to feel good on the inside, not just on the outside. At that time, I didn't know how to do that.

After that, I started working on my happiness. Before dancing, I was so focused on making *everyone else* happy. My breakdown over the social media rumors made me realize I needed to focus on *me*—so I wouldn't fall back into that dark place. Now that I'm older, I know not everyone understands mental health, and that's okay. But we should all try to be considerate of one another.

I finished freshman year with decent grades. I feel like I recovered well after skipping so much school, and I'm so glad I didn't drop out. I was starting to enjoy school again, loving the company of my friends, and doing great at the dance school. I really enjoyed Animal Science, especially Horse Management, since I grew up with horses. But I also fell in love with Landscaping, which completely changed my plan of studying Animal Science and becoming a vet. I ended up majoring in Plant Science.

In a way, I couldn't believe I was changing my path, especially since I was always the type of person that, once my mind was set, there was no turning back. But I was excited about this new direction. My first real job was working at Shaw's Supermarket in my hometown in the floral department. I enjoyed working with flowers and learning how to do arrangements, but at the time, I was still focused on becoming a vet in the military. I did love seeing the smiles on people's faces when they came to pick up flowers, though.

I was so serious about my vet plan that I quit my job at Shaw's two weeks before starting high school. I told my boss I wanted to focus on my future career and school since I wouldn't be in town anymore. So much for that idea!

During the summer between freshman and sophomore year, I started driver's education, and I loved it. It was another taste of freedom. I was more excited than most kids about getting my license because, growing up with seizures, I was always told it was up in the air whether I'd even be allowed to drive. There were extra hoops I had to jump through, but I did everything my parents, neurologist, and pediatrician told me to do.

Now, let's talk about the conversation no one wants to have—because, let's face it, that's what I do.

Epilepsy.

First things first, I am NOT a doctor. This is NOT medical advice. This is just my experience. I hope this finds the right people, those who have or had epilepsy, so they don't feel as alone as I did.

Most people reading this book have probably met or known someone with epilepsy. I'll do my best to explain how it affects us.

Daily struggles:

We are ALWAYS tired. No matter how much we sleep. So please, stop telling us to go to bed earlier, try a new mattress, or get a different pillow.

Here's where my anxiety started: I learned about SUDEP (Sudden Unexplained Death in Epilepsy Patients) in my teens. At sixteen, that was terrifying. I found out I could have a seizure in my sleep and just never wake up.

When I was first diagnosed, fancy surgeries weren't a thing. Epilepsy used to be called "guess-a-lepsy" because doctors would just guess what to do next with your brain. And let's not forget that, until the mid-1900s, epilepsy was seen as demonic possession or, in some African cultures, as punishment for a past sin. Fun facts I picked up from sitting in neurologists' offices for over two decades.

Another daily struggle:

We are ALWAYS thinking about our worst seizure. Something will trigger the memory, and suddenly, we're reliving it. If the memory is bad enough, it might cause a panic attack—which, surprise, stress can trigger seizures. Yeah. A vicious cycle.

Medication:

Finding the right medication is brutal. I was lucky. My first medication, Zarontin, worked for me, and I was on it from diagnosis until my mid-twenties. The side effects sucked, but it kept me seizure-free.

When I started driving, I got cocky and skipped doses. That medication worked so well that my parents could immediately tell when I missed one. I felt great and thought, in my stupid teenage brain, I didn't need it as much as my doctor said.

Medication in general scares me. I had a friend (may the Gods rest his soul) who was on Keppra. It's known for its psychological side effects. After being on it for some time, he took his own life. I miss him every day. Even with all our medical advancements, we'll never fully understand some things. Approving a drug that causes so many mental health issues is something I personally will never understand.

Finding a good doctor:

This is another battle. The doctor I had since I was diagnosed finally retired, so I had to find someone new. I asked for recommendations, did my research, and picked a doctor close to home with decent reviews.

Before my first appointment, they asked me to do an EEG and bloodwork, which I did. When I met the doctor, he seemed fine. I told him I had been on Zarontin for years but, as I got older, it made me more tired. He suggested switching to the pill version instead of the liquid, which I agreed to. Then he told me something that didn't sit right.

"Because you're more at risk for seizures at night, you should take all three doses at once before bed."

That felt off. But I slipped back into my old mindset and just said, "Okay."

When I got home, I decided to take one pill for a few days, then move to two, then three. One pill? Fine. No nausea as long as I ate. Two pills? Not so fine.

After taking two pills together for the first time, I sat down, then laid down because something felt wrong. The room started spinning. When I opened my eyes, I was hallucinating. I saw a four-foot spider on my kitchen wall.

I freaked out and tried to stand, but my legs wouldn't work. I collapsed.

An ambulance took me to the hospital. They told me my stomach needed to be pumped—I had overdosed.

Zarontin overdose can cause respiratory failure, coma, and death.

I was terrified. And furious. I told the nurse my doctor instructed me to take all three doses at once. She said she was relieved I hadn't. If I had taken the full dose, I wouldn't be here to tell my story.

This happened in 2014. Over ten years later, it still haunts me.

So why the detour into my epilepsy?

Because I want current and former epilepsy patients to know they are NOT alone. The fears, the feelings, the struggles—you're not the only one going through it.

As a woman, I also understand the added fear of pregnancy. The extra precautions. The medication risks.

I also talked about this because I went YEARS without feeling heard. I walked out of doctor's offices with more questions than answers. I want every survivor to know: I **HEAR YOU. I SEE YOU.**

Always advocate for yourself. Whether it's a doctor, an employer, or a stranger—don't lose your voice. Don't let someone make you do something that puts you in danger.

Okay, now back to my original story.

I entered sophomore year feeling good—about my friends, school, family, and dance. Things were finally on the upswing. I got my license a few days after my birthday in October, and I felt free as a bird.

I joined the outing club, where we planned ski trips. I started playing softball again and signed up for Ultimate Frisbee, which was way cooler than I expected.

Sophomore year was a blast. I had great grades and was thriving in Plant Science. But now I had another decision to make—what direction did I want to take for junior year?

My options: Floriculture, Horticulture, or Natural Resources.

I didn't want to rush into a choice and end up stuck in a class I hated. I asked upperclassmen and teachers about each major. I had an idea of what I wanted, but I wasn't sure.

I loved the science side—soil and water testing. But I also loved running equipment. My choice came down to Natural Resources or Horticulture.

I decided to do Natural Resources for my Junior and Senior years. I really enjoyed it. I still got to run equipment and chainsaws, but at the same time, I was able to do soil and water testing. I feel like I made the right decision because I loved what I was doing. I realized I should try everything and see what I liked. I was young and had time to change my mind if I wanted to.

At the time, I was working at a plant nursery. I wanted every edge I could get to be the best at what I was doing. I learned a lot of plant names, both common and scientific. I also learned how to do sales and sometimes ran the skid steer to help unload and load trucks for deliveries. I really enjoyed this job—the work and the people I worked with. My boss was one of the nicest people I had ever met, and she did everything she could to help me succeed. My goal was to be as well-rounded and versatile as possible.

One of my teachers approached me about an engineering contest. They thought I would be a strong candidate, so I looked into it. The contest was for high school juniors and seniors to design a bridge using a computer program. The goal was to test how it would hold up against different weighted vehicles and natural disasters. I worked on my bridges for weeks until I was happy with my design. I was proud of it. I submitted my entry and waited. I was competing against hundreds, if not thousands, of students across the country, many of whom I assumed were smarter than me.

Three weeks later, my school received a letter from the contest organizers—I won second place and $100. If I had still been in a depressed state of mind or had listened to the boys (and girls) back in elementary and middle school, I would have never entered. I would have continued to dumb myself down for others' enjoyment.

I see things on social media now—Facebook, Instagram, TikTok—where girls take quizzes like "Take this test to see how boys see you." This is one reason I believe women are losing their voices. And here's something no one wants to hear—parents don't want to parent anymore. They want to be their kids' friends. Fewer parents are teaching their children to think for themselves, to be strong and resilient. As a result, young girls believe these online quizzes and change themselves to fit what a quiz tells them they should be.

When I was little, my parents taught me to listen to people but take what they said with a grain of salt (depending on who it was, of course). They taught me that when someone points a finger at you, they have three fingers pointing back at themselves. They encouraged me to do what made me happy and to always have a voice, though they reminded me that there was a time and place for everything.

I am new to the writing world, and I am enjoying every minute of it. But when I first started talking to publishing companies before deciding to self-publish, I discovered an odd expectation. I was asked where I was writing my book. I answered, "In my house, in a small town outside of Boston." That was apparently the wrong answer. They meant, "Do you have a studio, a nook, or a 'writing room'?" I didn't even know that was a thing.

Let me paint you a picture: I'm sitting in bed in my pajamas, wearing an American Military University hoodie, half-watching Paw Patrol with my four-year-old, eating Smartfood popcorn. There is nothing glamorous about my writing process. But I had no problem saying that. I could have easily lied, saying, "Yes, I have a beautiful 1,100 sq. ft. suite where I sip wine while I write." I mean, I do have a 1,100 sq. ft. suite, but that's where I ran my construction company, and I don't like wine. We don't make millions a year. We don't send our daughter to an elite private school. We are a laid-back family.

Junior year, I was still playing varsity softball. I maintained high honors and ran track and cross-country, which helped me make more friends. Junior year was the highlight of my high school career. I loved my major, was excelling in academics, and was becoming comfortable with myself. The downside? I was introduced to harsh rumors.

I went on a date with a classmate—nothing major. We had dinner, watched a movie, and then I went home. We didn't even take the same vehicle. By Monday morning, rumors were swirling that I had slept with him or spent the night at his house. When I found out the rumors came from him, I confronted him immediately. I asked why he would start such lies. We didn't even kiss, and honestly, even if there hadn't been rumors, there wouldn't have been a second date.

I didn't take it well. Part of me wanted to say, "Yeah, sure, we slept together, but guess what? He sucks in bed and has nothing to brag about." But I didn't because that would have made me just as bad as him. I knew the truth, and so did my best friends. The good thing about high school? Every week, there's a new rumor. I'm glad I wasn't petty. It would have dragged things on, and I didn't want to be anyone's talking point. I wanted to have fun, make memories with my friends, and, oh yeah, get good grades. Sometimes, it's best to let things blow over. I noticed that when I didn't react how people expected, they seemed upset that I wasn't mad. Strange, but whatever.

Halfway through my Junior year, one of my teachers told me about the Student Conservation Association (SCA). They believed I was a strong student with leadership potential and good grades and encouraged me to apply. My parents and I researched the program, and they gave me their blessing. I had to pick three locations where I would live and work at a national park for most of the summer between Junior and Senior year. My first pick was Montana (Yellowstone), second was Alaska (Glacier Bay), and third was Hawaii (Kaloko-Honokōhau).

I sent my application and waited. Five or six weeks later, I got a letter. I waited for my parents to get home before opening it. I tore into it like it was Christmas morning, expecting to see "You're going to Hawaii." Instead, it said, "Pack your bags, you're heading to Roan Mountain, Tennessee, to work on the Appalachian Trail." Talk about a plot twist! But I was still excited.

For the next three months, I trained and prepared. I needed to carry 60 pounds on my back while hiking up to five miles. My friends loaded my school backpack with the heaviest stuff they could find, and I walked around campus with it. I was ready—terrified, but ready.

When it was finally time to go, I boarded my first flight from Boston to Charlotte, North Carolina. While waiting for my next flight, I saw three girls loaded with gear. I stood up, hoping they were my crew. Before I left, I learned I would be leading the first all-female crew in the program's 50-year history. That letter had been one of the most empowering moments of my life. Seeing the girls walking toward me, packed and ready to go, made it even more real.

We introduced ourselves, shared laughs, and boarded the tiny plane to our big adventure. Once we landed, we waved at the live camera feed pointed at the runway. Our parents probably couldn't see us, but it was the thought that counted. We met our SCA leaders and waited for one more girl, who was flying in from California.

After she arrived, we all piled into a van and headed for the mountain. The adventure was about to begin.

When we were driving to the mountain, we figured there was a road that would take us up to our cabin—maybe a van or some ATVs. We were so wrong. We got out of the van and met the kind older couple who owned the cabin where we were staying. They also lived in a cabin at the base of the mountain, and they would be responsible for holding onto our electronics. Any mail we needed to send or receive would go through their house first since our cabin didn't have an actual address.

We started looking around for transportation up the mountain. Want to know what was taking us up? Our feet. There was no transportation. So, we began our hike around 7:00 PM, each of us carrying two heavy backpacks. This was not what we expected. After hours in airports and long waits, we were exhausted and moving at a snail's pace. About halfway up, it was completely dark. The only light we had came from the battery-powered flashlights in our backpacks. Being on the side of a mountain, unsure of our exact location, was terrifying—especially since our phones were at the bottom. We had all heard the haunting stories about the Appalachian Trail, and hiking in the dark was not our idea of fun. We finally made it to our cabin around 11:00 PM. None of us cared to unpack. We rolled out our sleeping bags and went straight to sleep.

The next morning, our first full day on the mountain, we unpacked and then walked the trail to see where we would be working. Seeing the condition of the trail firsthand was eye-opening. We were expected to clear three miles—removing stumps, cutting back branches, and grading rough sections to prevent tripping hazards. The problem? We had no heavy equipment. Just hand tools. I had no idea about everyone's work ethic or if anyone had experience with labor-intensive work. I wasn't sure what I had gotten myself into, but I was here, and I had to make it work.

After surveying the trail, we returned to our cabin, cooking our food over a fire or a small propane stove. I was someone who never tried new foods. I knew what I liked and assumed what I didn't. But on this trip, I realized I had to be open-minded—or go hungry. So, I tried tofu. To this day, I still love it. I had promised myself that I would embrace new experiences—food, friends, and everything in between. That night, we sat around with flashlights and candles, talking. We had to be on the same page to get this job done. After discussing everyone's strengths and weaknesses, I put together a game plan. That's when the adventure truly began.

I won't recount every single day, but this trip was a turning point in my life. We had three "town days" during our month in Tennessee. These were our chances to explore, go out to eat, do laundry, and enjoy the scenery and shops. Our trip was set for thirty-six days—thirty-six days to complete three miles of trail, work with people I had never met before, and prepare for my senior year.

Around day twenty-nine, we headed into town and met with DCR. We expected bad news—delays due to rain or maybe extra work. Instead, we got a surprise: in twenty-nine days, we had completed 4.8 miles! We were told to enjoy our remaining days and explore. I had never felt prouder—of my crew for working so hard and of myself for stepping up as a leader. We visited Roan Plateau, which had a breathtaking view, then Twisting Falls. We even hiked the very trail we had spent nearly a month restoring.

With only three days left, we were living our best lives. We packed snacks and food, then set off on the trail. Along the way, we saw a mother bear with her cub and countless deer. After a few hours, we found another plateau where we sat, ate, and reflected on the past month. Looking back, I treasure the fact that I didn't have my phone. Without it, I was fully present. The only pictures I appeared in were a few group shots taken by our leaders. Part of me wishes I had more, but I know I would've been glued to my phone instead of truly experiencing everything.

After sitting on the plateau for a couple of hours, we packed up and continued our hike. We reached the top of the mountain, took in the view, then started heading back. Down the trail, we spotted a stream and decided to cross it by stepping from stone to stone. That's when everything changed. I stepped wrong, my foot slipped, and I went down—hard. Not only was I soaked, but I couldn't put any weight on my foot. We were still a 30-minute walk from the cabin. One of our leaders called the couple at the bottom of the mountain. They arrived about forty-five minutes later with a four-seat ATV. I was told they'd take me to the bottom, where I'd get my phone to call my mom before heading to the hospital. The ride down was bumpy and painful, but hearing my mom's voice gave me peace of mind. I'll never forget her joking, "Don't forget, you're in rural Tennessee on the side of a mountain—they're probably taking you to a vet." I laughed, but I couldn't help thinking, she might not be wrong.

At the hospital, they did imaging, and I expected to be told to ice it and rest. Instead, they told me I had torn ligaments and needed to go home to see a specialist. I was devastated. I had only three days left. I had to call my mom and arrange an early flight home. That night, I returned to the cabin on crutches. The girls were happy I was back—until I told them I was leaving the next day. We spent the night by the fire, reminiscing. We exchanged phone numbers and promised to keep in touch. For many years, we did. But life happens, and most of us lost touch. This trip had been the biggest thing I had ever done. I was on cloud nine, but I wasn't ready to leave. I wanted us all to finish together—as a team.

The morning came, and I packed my things. The van was on its way. I had an hour to say my goodbyes. One of the girls asked if they could all come to the airport with me. Thankfully, our leaders said yes. When we arrived, the girls helped me with my bags, we exchanged hugs, and then I was wheeled to my gate. Before my flight, I texted everyone so they'd have my number once they got their phones back. Then, I boarded my plane and started my journey home.

When I landed in Boston, my mom was there waiting. The moment I saw her, I cried. She wheeled me to the car, and I was in for a surprise—while I was gone, she had bought a new car and gotten her first tattoo. What the hell had happened while I was away? I was so happy to be back on Massachusetts soil, reunited with my family and friends. Exhausted, I took my pain meds and went to sleep.

Then, another surprise: the local newspaper wanted to interview me. My school had contacted them about my trip. Within days, they came to take pictures, so my big debut was me—on crutches, with an air cast. Not what I expected, but

I still have the original article to this day. My parents also threw a welcome home party with all my friends and family. Despite being stuck on crutches, I made the best of it.

Senior year had finally arrived, and I was ready. I had just completed the biggest accomplishment of my life, and I was so proud. Even better news? My neurologist was starting to wean me off my seizure medication. Many people with my type of epilepsy grow out of it by eighteen. By mid-September, we began adjusting my dosages. It was one less thing to worry about—and the next chapter of my life was about to begin.

I turned eighteen on October 5th, 2006. The weaning process was going well—I wasn't having seizures, I was less tired, I could focus better, and I was living my best life in my senior year of high school. Things couldn't have been better! My favorite thing in the world was climbing trees. I was one of the best climbers in my class—fast, skilled, and able to tie any knot I was asked to. I was a pro at running a chainsaw, whether on the ground or in the air. My whole life revolved around work. I earned the nickname "Squirrel," and I felt on top of the world.

Then everything came to a screeching halt.

I probably shouldn't have been climbing trees so soon after coming back—I was still on crutches—but I relied more on my core muscles than my legs anyway. On October 17th, 2006, I was doing tree work near the main office building. Everything was going smoothly. By that point, I was down to a quarter of my usual dose, taking only one pill a day at lunchtime. Within another week, I'd be completely off my medication.

I was on the ground, watching a friend up in the tree pruning branches to clear a higher climbing path. I spotted her for about twenty-five minutes before my teacher told me to get my harness on and head up. I geared up, threw my ropes, and climbed up to where my friend was. She swung to the other side of the tree, and we both got to work. About ten minutes later, I suddenly felt hot and dizzy.

Next thing I knew, I was falling back in my harness, convulsing, and then going limp—with a running chainsaw hanging off me.

My friend shut her chainsaw off and helped my teacher get me back to the ground from about fifteen feet in the air. I don't remember any of it. Everything I know comes from my classmates and teacher. They told me I was laid in the bed of a Gator 6-wheeler and driven to the nurse's office. There, I was put on a bed, and my friends refused to leave my side.

I stared at my two best friends, repeatedly asking who they were and where I was. The nurse called my mom, who came to get me immediately.

At the hospital, they did blood work and checked me over. My mom explained that I was at the end of my medication weaning process. A few hours later, we got a call from my neurologist. I was told to stay home and lay low until further tests came back and they could hook me up to an EEG.

I got my blood work done and went in for the EEG. A few days later, I returned to school. We were off-campus by the Ipswich River doing water testing when my cell phone rang. My teacher saw it was my doctor and let me step away to take the call. I walked over by a tree, looking at my friends and giving them a thumbs-up, thinking I was in the clear. I still wasn't 100%, my memory was off, but I was excited to be back.

The conversation with my doctor started fine. He asked how I was feeling and if I was back at school. I told him the truth—I still had memory issues and felt weak, but I was there. Then he dropped the bomb: "Due to your seizure, I have to put you back on medication."

That stung, but I could deal with it. I'd been on medication for twelve years—what was another six months? But then he gave me the worst news: "I need you to turn in your license for six months. No equipment or climbing for six months."

At that moment, I was furious. I whipped my phone across the trail and sat down, crying. My friends ran over, asking what was wrong. I told them. My world felt like it had crashed. Senior year was supposed to be my time. I was an upperclassman. I had done my time as a lowerclassman and didn't need to do grunt work anymore. Now I was being forced to drag brush with freshmen.

Depression hit me like an elephant on my chest. I started cutting again. I experimented with "road sodas" at school. I stopped caring about everything. I couldn't go out on work-study since I couldn't use equipment. I got a job at Bob's Clothing Store, just to have some income, but I hated it. After three weeks, I started sleeping through shifts. I even got detentions just to avoid going to work.

Winter was miserable. My memory was still shot, and I barely made it through midterms. I had to endure this hell until April, meaning I only had two months left to enjoy my senior year.

In February, we were told about a job fair in mid-April. That finally lifted my spirits. These employers didn't know me or my situation, and by the time I landed a job, I'd be off "lockdown." I took a business class where we learned to write cover letters, resumes, and business plans. In March, my teachers eased me back into using smaller equipment and climbing again. I was excited, training one-on-one with my climbing teacher.

Two weeks before the job fair, I put my harness on for the first time since October. I grabbed my rope, but when I looked at it, I froze. I had forgotten how to tie in.

That broke me. Five months ago, I could tie in with my eyes closed. I spent the next week practicing knots at school and at home. I refused to give up. When Monday came, I was ready. I climbed six feet, then panicked. Flashbacks hit me—the feeling of dangling, my doctor's words echoing in my head. I climbed down, threw my gear in my bag, and walked away.

At lunch, I found my teacher and told him I wanted to try again. He asked if I was sure. I was. That afternoon, I told him, "I'm not taking this harness off or leaving until I climb this tree." After 40 minutes of climbing a little higher each time, I finally reached 25 feet. I reset my ropes, went higher, grabbed my hand saw, and got to work. For the first time in months, I felt like myself again.

The job fair arrived. I dressed my best, with a binder containing my resume, cover letter, work photos, transcripts, and recommendations. I sat down with a tree company owner, but when I mentioned epilepsy, he ripped my resume in half and said, "Not interested. Next." At the next company, I was told, "We don't hire women—too many problems." That day, I realized how brutal this industry could be.

Feeling defeated, I sat at the next table—a country club hiring for groundskeeping. The interviewer was soft-spoken and genuinely interested in my skills. That moment became the start of three things: my first real job in the industry, a lifelong friendship, and a mentorship.

By April, I got my license and started work-study at the country club. But the industry exposed me to a lot. One day, while driving a mower back to the shop, I spotted movement near the woods. I assumed it was a deer—until I looked closer and saw my co-workers using drugs and engaging in "adult activities." I kept my mouth shut and moved on.

Prom came and went. I cut greens that morning with royal blue and white acrylic nails, then got ready for the big night.

I fell into the wrong crowd. I dated an older guy who treated me like garbage. The final straw? When someone asked how he landed me, he said, "She clearly has low self-esteem." He wasn't wrong. Years of bullying made me cling to anyone who showed kindness, even if it was fake.

Then came my dream—enlisting in the Marines. But epilepsy got me declined. I never even told my parents I tried. Feeling lost, I applied to colleges and got accepted across the country. Despite all I had overcome, I still felt insecure.

Graduation came on June 7th, 2007—the day before my dad's birthday. I had fought through seizures, depression, rejection, and doubt. And I made it. I was ready for whatever came next.

Chapter 3

College

There is a quote about self-love that I really enjoy. It's from Alan Cohen, and it says, "To love yourself right now, just as you are, is to give yourself to heaven. Don't wait until you die. If you wait, you die now. If you love, you live now." I agree wholeheartedly with this quote; it really hits hard every time I see it.

Like I said, I had no reason to feel so insecure, but I was. With everything that I did, I still am very insecure to this day. One of my biggest problems—this stems from when I was much younger, though I didn't realize how bad it was until I graduated high school and started college—was being a people pleaser. At least in the beginning, nothing was dangerous, but I had trouble saying "no" to people. I would constantly take on too much, and I didn't like to face conflict. Instead of feeding into it or confronting it—I guess that's a better way to describe it—I would shut down. I would stop answering.

College was also when I learned that I could be very vicious with my words. As I got older, I realized I had never really worked through my anger and depression. I kept stuffing my feelings down, which became another reason I would shut people out. I didn't want to say anything that would truly hurt someone, no matter how mad I was.

I entered North Shore Community College in September 2008, where I majored in Horticulture with a minor in Business Management. I enjoyed my classes, but I could have done and been so much more. I could have gone to any of those colleges I applied to for law or something else, but again, I sold myself short and went to a community college. Not that there's anything wrong with community college, but my reasoning for going there is embarrassing.

Since I majored in Horticulture in college and had attended Essex Aggie for high school, majoring in Natural Resources, I was able to skip seven or eight classes right away when I arrived at college. I took the effortless way out when I could have done so much more. I wouldn't change my life path for anything—everything I did became a life lesson. I had a lot of fun, but college is when I started experimenting more with different things. In a way, I started becoming someone I really was not proud of anymore.

So, when my editors read through these first few chapters, they really got a kick out of my "glamorous writing" descriptions in Chapter Two. I was told that in each chapter, I should pick a random spot and describe everything that's going on—that people would enjoy that. So, okay, here's a word picture of tonight's shit show:

I am currently sitting on the couch. It is 9:26 PM (EST). My daughter is fast asleep with her dog, Rebel. My husband is watching football (American football), and I am sitting here, as I said, on the couch, in my pajamas, listening to Native American flute music and eating popcorn. Yup, the glamor hasn't lost its sparkle yet.

I don't want my entire book to be about negative things in my life. I've lived a fantastic life, and I still am. My freshman year of college, I got my first job working for a landscaping company a few towns over. I worked in the maintenance department, caring for commercial properties with a crew of four people. I was the only female working in the field, and I was looked down on a lot. I was treated differently, even by the owners of the company.

Now, I want to talk about something quick—a very touchy subject: the wage gap.

When I started working there, I wanted to drop out of college. I was in school full-time Monday through Thursday, so Friday and Saturday were the only days I could work full-time in the field. The other days, I worked in the office, learning the business side of landscaping and construction. But I was making more money working. I was going to school on my own loans—my parents weren't helping me pay for it—so I figured it was my choice. I wanted to make more money and work more hours. I knew I could likely learn more working than I would just going to school and relearning things I had already learned in high school.

I made the owner of the company aware that I would be ready to work more hours soon, as I planned to finish the semester and then drop out to work full-time. I told her I wanted to make more money. She told me to stick it out and finish—there would be a "hefty raise" waiting for me after graduation.

After this conversation, I started getting treated even more differently than before. I had been at the company for about six months. I had earned my keep over the winter, got my hydraulics license and D.O.T., and did everything asked of me. The same crew I had been on since the beginning started putting in complaints about me. It wasn't a surprise that I couldn't lift as much as the guys on my crew. I never asked for help or for someone to do it for me, but instead of emptying my mower in two barrels like the guys, I had to use three barrels. That had never been an issue. But suddenly, six months in, it was a problem.

I was pulled from the maintenance department and told all I would be doing was planting flowers. That's great sometimes, but why did I push to get my degree so I could run a maintenance crew and operate a skid steer when needed, only to end up just planting flowers?

Do you want to know why I feel there is a wage gap? It's because of company owners who make empty promises.

I finished my associate's degree. I didn't even walk across the stage. I went, picked up my diploma at the school, and brought it to work. I walked into my boss's office, put it on her desk, and told her I was ready to go full-time.

I was told to take Thursday through Sunday off to enjoy graduation and spend time with my friends before going full-time. I thought I was going to walk in on Monday to the raise I was promised.

Instead, on Saturday, the mailman knocked on my door. He had certified mail for me. I signed for it, put it down, and finished getting ready. When I finally opened it, I read:

"We wanted to send you a letter to make you aware that we are going in a different direction with your employment."

Just like that, my job was gone.

I was furious. I tried calling everyone—straight to voicemail. So I drove to the office. When I walked in, everyone's jaws dropped, and they looked down. I asked where the owner was, and I was told she wasn't there. I held up the letter and asked, "Who else knew about this?" A girl stood up and said, "I'm sorry. We were told not to say anything."

That experience broke me, but I refused to roll over and give up.

Now, about the wage gap—I think this is a big reason it happens. Owners and managers make promises they can't keep. When things like this happen, people give up, lose their self-worth, and settle.

But here's the thing: STOP PLAYING THE WOMAN CARD. Get out there and work harder. Make people shut up. Stop saying, "I want this because I'm a woman" or "I don't get this because I'm a woman." Maybe that's true, but that's when you stand up and figure out what you need to do to make the money you want.

I've done college four times. I won't go into detail again, but each experience taught me something.

And let's be real—I still wouldn't hold a tarantula.

Chapter 4

Abuse

> **TRIGGER WARNING:** The following content contains themes that may be distressing or triggering to some individuals. Please proceed with care and prioritize your well-being.

Let me just say that what happened to me, which I speak of in this chapter, will be a massive trigger warning for most people. It is okay to skip this chapter—there are no hard feelings. I was a victim of assault at the hands of someone I worked with, and because of him, I began to abuse substances. These are days, weeks, months, and years of my life that I will never get back. He will never face justice how he should, and he will never feel remorse. But I can say that I am a survivor, and I can now share my story to help other people heal. After this happened, I realized I had the rest of my life to turn my mental health around and use evil for good.

I was struggling with life in general. I was not making good decisions, and I felt pushed against a wall, which led me to make even worse decisions. My parents had gotten divorced. I left home after a hefty fight with my mom. I was dating someone who treated me horribly—yet again. I felt like I was at a roadblock in life, and at this point, I didn't care what happened anymore. As always, I worked, but that was the only constant thing I had going for me.

Something I realize now that I am older—and I would like to think a little wiser—is that if you continue to allow a certain behavior, people will continue to do those behaviors because you allow it. It is all about setting boundaries, whether it is with your significant other, a friend, or a family member—it doesn't matter. Your mental health should not be risked for someone else's sake.

I was working at a different landscaping company. I was back to doing maintenance, so I was happy about that. I dated a kid I worked with, and sadly, even the guys I worked with were warning me about him. Naturally, I didn't listen, and this relationship changed my life forever. He was three years younger than I was, and he had a lot more problems.

I could see he had issues, but in the relationships I had been in before, I was abused mentally, financially, emotionally, and in some instances, physically. After going through all of that, my self-esteem was at an all-time low, and I didn't believe I deserved better than what I had.

First off, I didn't care what happened at this point. And second, as bad as it sounds, I was used to the abuse. I was one of those people who preached on Facebook about how I was a strong woman and that women need to know their worth. I would be telling my friends all this advice on how they need to be better versions of themselves, but I could not take my own advice. That is when my life got dangerous.

This kid I was dating was not safe at all. He drank heavily, did drugs, drove like he was racing, had bad anger issues, and was a narcissist. I remember when I met his parents—his dad told me, "As long as my kids only do hallucinogens, then that is fine, but no hard drugs." I should have left at that point and never looked back. But I think it was the thrill of the danger that made me stick around. What can I say? I was young and dumb.

He ended up breaking up with me because I was going to school for Criminal Justice. He told me, "I can't date a cop, not with how I live my life." I remember that day. We were in downtown Ipswich, MA, over by the train station. I was excited because I had been accepted into AMU for Criminal Justice. I told him how excited I was, and the conversation started with him telling me I was not smart enough to be a cop. He told me to just stick with landscaping because that's all I would be able to do.

I told him how, when I was younger, I just wanted to be a Marine. That's when he told me I was weak and wouldn't last a week in basic training. Then, when I told him my major was Criminal Justice and that I was going to take my environmental police exam, he got angry. He started asking if I was already a cop and if I was going to turn him in. He asked if I was wired up. He started to get crazy. Then he stopped talking, looked at me, gave me the finger, and said, "F*** the police and f*** the military."

He walked back to his car and took off down the street. I stood there for a second in total disbelief at what had just happened. Then I walked back to my truck and left.

We still, unfortunately, worked at the same company, but he worked in construction, and I worked in maintenance, so we very rarely saw each other. Everyone kept telling me, "He's a good worker, but you can do so much better. Don't worry about it."

A few weeks before Memorial Day, one of the other guys I worked with said, "Why don't we all head up to Hampton Beach for Memorial Day weekend?" At this point, my ex and I had been broken up for a few months. The sting of the breakup was over, so I said, "Sure, I'll go."

Memorial Day weekend that year changed my life forever. It was the first time I experienced real trauma. We all went to a karaoke bar right on the beach. We were all having a fun time, watching all the drunk people sing horribly for karaoke.

I remember one of the most important things my dad always taught me: never leave a drink unattended at a bar. If you must leave it for whatever reason, just throw it out. Well, for whatever reason, I thought I could trust the people I was with. But clearly, I couldn't.

When I went into the bathroom, I came back out, sat down at the bar, and had a sip of my drink. After about two or three minutes, I don't remember anything from the bar.

The next thing I remembered was waking up a few doors up the street at a motel, to my ex saying, "Okay, now I'm done, and you better not say anything... f****** cop wannabe." Then he left the room.

He left his room card on the table next to the bed. I rolled back over and cried. I felt dirty. I felt used. My self-esteem was so much lower than it had been before that. Finally, when I felt I was able to move, I got up, locked the door, and set the deadbolt. Then I sat down on the chair in the room and tried to remember how the hell I got there. I couldn't remember anything.

Eventually, I got up and left. At this point, it was 1 AM. I went downstairs and asked if there was a different room available so I could just sleep. The guy at the desk said there was one room available, so I said, "I'll take it."

He said, "It's a suite and a bit more expensive. Is that okay?"

I told him, "I don't care what the price is. I just need somewhere to lay down."

I grabbed the room key from the guy and headed upstairs. When I got into the room, I showered, then laid down, cried, and eventually went to sleep.

Not that I have to explain myself to anyone—because if a man can't control himself, that is not a me problem, that's definitely a him problem (and a society problem). But before people start jumping down my throat with, "What were you wearing? Were you asking for it?"—for anyone who doesn't know me, I am a T-shirt and jeans type of girl. I was wearing sneakers, flare jeans, a fitted T-shirt, and a backwards black baseball cap.

I woke up around 10:30 AM the next day and sat on the edge of the bed for a while. I had thirty minutes to burn until checkout and a hell of a walk back to my truck, which I was just hoping was still there at that point.

Even after sleeping that long, I still couldn't recall anything from the night before. I got up, showered one more time, then started my walk back to my truck.

When I made it back, I saw I had a parking ticket for being there overnight without a hotel voucher pass. At this point, that was fine—at least my truck was still there, and I was alive.

The part that got me was that everyone I worked with made me feel like they were looking out for me, telling me to leave this guy. But when whatever happened, happened, not one of them tried to call or text me. No note was left on my truck. Nothing. I was alone. I survived, but I was alone.

I went home and went right back to sleep. I was not looking forward to work on Tuesday and seeing him. I made up my mind before I went to sleep that I would give my two weeks' notice when I got to work on Tuesday—then likely call out sick for two weeks. I saw that as the only way to get away from this.

Tuesday morning rolled around. I drove into work and parked. I sat in my truck for a short time and took a few deep breaths. I not only had to face my ex, but I had to try to hold back from punching every one of them in the face. It was my own fault for making myself that vulnerable, but I was still mad at them for not even texting or calling me to make sure I was okay.

I felt like I couldn't tell anyone what happened. To this day, the only people who know what happened that night are my brother (who found out in 2022) and my two best friends (who I didn't tell until three or four years after it happened).

I walked into the yard to grab my paperwork for the day and started walking toward the office to give my two weeks' notice when one of the guys stopped me and pulled me aside.

He said, "What happened the other night?"

I said, "I'm pretty sure you know what happened."

He said, "_____ came back to the bar and said you had left—that you had one of your friends pick you up to go home."

I didn't even know what to say at that point. All I could muster up was, "That's not even close to what happened to me that night."

I went to walk away, and he grabbed me by the arm and said, "You know he got arrested, right?"

I looked at him and asked, "What was he arrested for?"

He proceeded to tell me he was arrested for DUI when he finally left the bar. My jaw hit the ground.

First of all, after what he did to me, he actually went back to the bar and kept partying. Who does that?

I still gave my two weeks' notice that day. And even now, unless that monster told the guys at some point, the people we worked with have no idea what happened that weekend.

I found another job and worked my two weeks. I found out that he was released from jail and got a different job as well.

I started my new job, and I was liking it.

With this being the first time I had ever really had true trauma in my life, I was not sure how to handle all of this. I kept everything quiet and moved through life as best as I could.

I put myself into therapy, but for whatever reason, I could not talk about it with my therapist. I spoke about smaller problems going on in my life. I spoke about my parents' divorce and how I felt about it. I spoke about work. But I never spoke about the assault.

I never went to the police, either. When I heard he was arrested for DUI, I figured that was it—he would be locked away, and I wouldn't have to worry about him anymore. That was not the case.

It was like I couldn't live normally after that. Men in general made me nervous. The only men I could be around were my father and my brothers. I had panic attacks when I stayed at hotels, and I didn't return to Hampton Beach for about five years.

I suffered in silence for an exceedingly long time.

A couple of years after everything happened to me, I built up the courage to say something to the police. I called ahead and told them I wanted to file a sexual assault complaint and speak with a detective. They told me the detective would be in the next day and gave me a time to show up.

The next day, I pulled into the parking lot and sat there for about 30 minutes, just looking at the building. An officer walked up to the passenger side of my truck and knocked on the window, scaring the hell out of me. I rolled the window down, and he asked if I was okay. I told him I was just trying to build up the courage to go inside for my meeting with the detective. He was very nice and asked if I needed him to walk me inside. But even years later, I didn't trust any man, so I politely said, "No, thank you," got out of my truck, and went inside.

I told the front desk who I was and who I was meeting with, and they told me to take a seat. I was sweating bullets at this point. My stomach was turning, and I wanted to throw up.

I was called back to the office, and I cried before I even started talking.

I told the detective everything that happened to me. But when I told them when it happened, they seemed to check out of the conversation. Then they asked why I waited so long to speak up. I looked at them and cried. I told them I honestly didn't know why I waited as long as I did. I guess it was partially because I didn't know how to deal with my emotions. I didn't know how to tell people what happened to me. I knew he got arrested that night, and I guess I tried to lie to myself and tell myself it was because someone had told the police what he did to me and that I was safe.

The detective took the report and told me they would keep me posted.

A few days later, I finally got a call.

Long story short, I was told there was nothing they could do, that I should not have put myself into a situation like I did, and that I should not have been hanging out with an ex-boyfriend.

I didn't even know what to say at that point. I just said, "Okay, thank you for your time," and I hung up.

I was already emotionally drained from what happened a few years back, and now I was extra drained from knowing for sure that he was not going to face justice for what he did to me. And it was my fault he wouldn't face justice because I didn't speak up.

I went home and called out of work for about a week, saying I had a stomach bug and that I would be back in a week or so.

Since then, I have healed—but not fully. I will never fully heal from what I went through that summer.

I did take a few lessons from this experience.

First and foremost, my father was right—don't trust anyone at the bar. Had I listened, I would have come back from the bathroom, thrown my beer away, gotten a new one, and never would have gotten drugged or been in the situation I was in.

Second, I should not have kept my mouth shut for as long as I did. I should have stopped lying to myself and gone to the police the next day to make him face the authorities.

Third, it took years for me to come to terms with the fact that I put myself in that situation—but it was NOT my fault that a grown man could not control himself and attacked me by means of drugs.

Lastly, this is, unfortunately, why people—and I say people because it happens to men too (not as much, but it does happen)—do not speak up. Whether it's friends, family, or authorities, someone always has something to say, and more often than not, nothing is done.

I promised myself that after all my soul-searching and healing, I would use whatever platform I have to let people know:

I hear you.

And I am here for you.

Chapter 5

Drugs and Drinking

"Those events that once made me feel ashamed and disgraced now allow me to share with others how to become a useful member of the human race." This is a quote from what I call the "Bible of AA," but to most people, it is known as *The Big Book*. If you are struggling with sobriety, invest in *The Big Book*; you will not be disappointed.

I took my first sip of alcohol when I was about fourteen years old. It was a sip of wine, and I hated the taste (to this day, I am not a fan of wine), but I liked how it made me feel. I felt almost more confident; it made me feel warm. I remember my mom telling me that alcoholism and addiction ran in the family, on both her side and my dad's. When I drank, all those insecurities seemed okay. Whatever I was feeling that made me not feel good about myself, alcohol calmed me down. At that young age, I saw it as fixing the problem, not just throwing a band-aid on it. When the same problems arose again, I saw them as new, not the same ones I kept pushing down. I listened to what I was told, but I never thought it would happen to me. I never thought I had an addictive personality, but I was so wrong.

After that first sip, I tried more whenever I had the chance. At this point, I was not hooked. I was not a daily drinker by any means, but I saw alcohol as something that helped, not harmed, and that made it dangerous. My mental health was suffering. In the late '90s and early 2000s, mental health help was not really a thing, so any problems I had were pushed down and overlooked. It was no fault of my parents; it was just how things were at that time.

I tried drinking here and there in high school—at dances and parties. It was fun, but I did not feel hooked at that point. When I went on my trip to Tennessee, I obviously did not bring anything with me. While I was there, I was just high on life. I made myself proud, my family proud, and, in the grand scheme of things, I made my school proud as well. I was the first student from The Aggie to do a trip like this. On top of that, I ran the first all-female crew in the existence of the SCA.

Alright, before I dive deep into my severe problems, let's take everyone's favorite break—my glamorous word picture.

I am sitting in my office, wearing a dark purple Snuggie with the hood up. My husband just called me "Grimace." My dog is lying under my desk and just ripped a fart that is slowly killing me. Bet you're really enjoying that one, right? Okay, moving on...

When the injury happened in Tennessee, and I was told I would need to go home early, my depression set back in—not just insecurities, but real depression. When I got home and met with a doctor in Boston, I was put on pain medication. That was a whole different feeling. Yes, it did what it was supposed to do—it numbed the pain of the injury—but it also numbed me in general. I felt like I was floating. That's when the problems started. I finished what the doctor gave me and tried to move forward.

I graduated high school and went on to work and do my thing in college. I got injured my freshman year when I was crushed between a house and a mower catcher. My ribs and hip were killing me. I ended up at urgent care per my boss's orders, where they did an X-ray. There were no broken ribs, thankfully, but they figured my ribs were bruised. I was handed pain pills, sent home, and told to rest. I was given a note to stay out of work for at least a week and, when I returned, to only do light-duty tasks for another week. I began taking the pills more often than I should have. I was meant to take them every four to six hours, but I took them every one to two hours. The way I saw it, there was nothing wrong with this. It was prescribed to me, so what I was doing had to be okay. I was taking something a professional gave me.

As I got older and turned twenty-one, I began going out drinking with my friends. When I got home, I would take a pill or two and crash for the night. At the time, I didn't see anything wrong with what I was doing. I was still going to work. I was earning money. My bills were paid with no help from anyone. I was independent and self-sufficient. I did this for a year, and somehow, I was functioning enough to keep my job.

After what happened to me at Hampton Beach, you would think I would have slowed down on going out and partying. I didn't. I actually did the complete opposite. I partied harder because I was so depressed and anxious. If I didn't feel like going out, that was fine. I could drink and do pills at home. I didn't see this as a big deal. I actually saw it as something safer. At least I was home. No one could hurt me there—except for me.

In 2014, I went to the hospital for severe stomach pain. They ran tests and told my dad I had acute appendicitis. They sent me home with pain medications and told me to rest. Twenty-four hours later, I went to a different hospital, still in pain. They ran more tests and told my mom I had acute appendicitis. Again, I was sent home with more pain medication. After what happened with that neurologist, I didn't have much trust in doctors anymore, especially with major things. I continued to take the pills and was in and out of work because of the pain. About eight or nine days later, I was at work when I picked up a barrel of leaves to throw in the back of the dump truck. As soon as I got the barrel over my head, I fell to the ground. My coworkers unhooked the trailer and drove me to the hospital. There, I was told I needed surgery to remove my appendix. I didn't quite understand, so I said, "Okay, I can come back tomorrow and do the surgery." The nurse looked at me and said, "No, you don't understand. You're staying. You're having surgery now."

That surgery, my addiction, my struggles with mental health, and the loss of my brother all played a role in where I ended up. I was self-medicating. I was numbing my pain. But ultimately, I was on the road to destruction. It took nearly losing everything—including my life—to realize I needed to change. My sobriety date is December 7, 2017. To this day, I am free from pills and continue to take control of my life.

I hope my story helps someone else realize they are not alone. Sobriety is a journey, and it's not easy. But it's worth it. If sharing my struggles can help even one person, then every hardship was worth it.

Sobriety is not an easy ride. Even though you're doing something good for your mental and physical health, there will be people who put you down for going to AA or NA. Some judge it based on its reputation, while others simply don't understand how the program works. I used to be one of those people who believed addiction was a choice, not a disease. I was wrong. For a long time, I thought it was my choice to pick up a bottle and chase it with pills.

When I hit my one-year anniversary, I felt untouchable. I got my medallion, and the next day was the company Christmas party—held at the same place where I had my last drunk. I walked in feeling strong, empowered, and confident in my sobriety. I ordered a soda and some food, but as everyone around me started ordering drinks, I felt the pull. I was having fun, but at the same time, I saw the alcohol, and I wanted it. The strange part? I didn't just want to drink—I wanted to mix it with pills.

The past few weeks had been incredibly stressful. I was a foreman at a landscaping company, short-staffed, trying to close out the season. My relationship at the time was a dumpster fire. I had a lot on my plate. I left the party early, got into my truck, and cried. That's when I truly understood: addiction is not a choice. It's a disease.

Since getting sober in December 2017, I've worked on my mental health. I've confronted my issues and had breakthroughs that helped me understand why I abused my body the way I did. Sobriety doesn't erase stress—it just teaches you how to deal with it properly. I now see that I used substances to cope with the abusive relationships I was in. I didn't know how to sit with my feelings, whether they were happy or sad. I was taught to push them down, and in my relationships, my feelings were dismissed altogether.

I'm far from perfect, and I still struggle some days. But the difference is, I can now sit with my emotions. I've learned coping mechanisms that work for me. I am no longer controlled by an overbearing partner who dictated my every move.

If you're on the journey of sobriety—whether from alcohol, pills, or drugs—know that your fears are valid, and most of us have them. Find what works for you and hold onto it. Even if your family doesn't support or understand your journey, there are people out there who do. Find your people. Keep explaining your struggles to those who matter. Eventually, they'll come around—and when they do, they'll have your back.

Don't Play the Woman Card

Chapter 6

Working

I always heard, "Love what you do, and you will never work a day in your life." I did love what I did for work; it was dealing with other people that I had a problem with. When I chose to enter this field back in 2002, working at the supermarket in the Florist Department, I had high hopes. As I moved through high school, I gained confidence in my work. For the most part, I was treated well by the people teaching me, so I developed an unrealistic vision of what working in this field would be like.

I had already talked about what happened at my first job working for that landscaping company. The next company I worked for, I started as a crew member. I worked my ass off for seven months, earned a raise, and secured a spot in a plow truck for the winter. I was excited and felt like I had accomplished something. My licenses and schooling were finally being recognized, and it felt amazing.

About halfway through the winter, I had a meeting with the owner. We sat down, and I was told how great my work was, how clients were leaving great reviews, and how the company was thriving. I was told that going into the next season, I would start with more money and be promoted to crew leader, running my own crew. The next season began, and I felt great. One of the other crew leaders took me along with him for a few weeks to show me exactly what a crew leader was supposed to do. I took notes on all the properties, special client requests, and any tips and tricks he could give me.

About four months into my position, a few guys had an issue taking orders from a female, but I had anticipated that. As annoying as it was, I didn't let it bother me much. A few months in, the owner hired a few guys on visas because we were overloaded with work. They had temp contracts just for the season. I took one of them with me to train, while the other crew leader took the other new guy. On the way to the property, I asked him some questions to get to know him—about his experience, if he had kids, a wife, his hobbies—just small talk to pass the time. He proceeded to tell me he had thirteen kids and liked to sleep with white women because if he had kids here, he had a better chance of staying in America.

I looked at him and said, "So you don't have a wife?" He responded, "I do, she is back in my country, but I need to get my green card." At that point, I felt extremely uncomfortable and pissed off that he was so relaxed about telling me something like that. I texted the other crew leader around lunchtime, told him about the conversation, and asked if we could switch. He agreed. I finished my day with the guy and went home.

The next day, I took the other new guy with me. He seemed more experienced and didn't say anything inappropriate, making for a much better day. Around lunchtime, the owner checked in, and I told him everything was going great. After lunch, we got back on the road. I pulled onto the highway, heading to the next property, when suddenly, this guy—who I had just given a great report about—reached over and grabbed my chest. In one swift movement, I put my knee on the wheel, grabbed his hand with my left, and punched him with my right. I pulled the truck and trailer to the side of the highway and called the owner, telling him what had just happened. I told him I left the guy on the side of the highway and that someone else could go get him. I was so shaken up that I took the next day off.

When I returned, my boss called a crew meeting. He announced that his wife was divorcing him and that he would have to sell the business at the end of the season. I was in shock. When everyone parted, I confronted him. That's when I found out the guy who assaulted me had called the office—knowing the owner's wife worked there—and falsely claimed her husband was sleeping with a female employee. I quit on the spot. As I walked past the guy who did this, I shoved him into the side of the truck and kicked him between the legs. He fell, called me a "b****," and I knelt down, saying, "That's a big word for someone on the ground crying. Touch me again, I dare you."

This was just another roadblock. I was a hard worker, and all I wanted was to use my licenses and be appreciated.

Everyone's favorite section, "Glamorous Word Picture." This one is far from glamorous. I'm sitting on the couch, eating a sandwich. My daughter is at school, my husband is at work, and I'm not feeling well, so I'm home. My hair is in a ponytail, I'm still in pajamas, and I feel far from glamorous. Onward…

I spent the next few days job hunting and found a promising opportunity. Things went well—I got a company vehicle, loved the properties I maintained, and this job opened doors for me in criminal justice. I gained the confidence to take the

Environmental Police Exam, and I passed. But when the time came to take the leap, I didn't feel ready. I wasn't confident enough to leave my comfort zone.

I passed the exam but was told that current officers and military personnel would be prioritized. Another setback. I visited my mom, who had made a cake celebrating my achievement. I was happy she acknowledged my success, but depression crept in because I knew I wouldn't be an Environmental Officer. I ate my cake, thanked my mom, and went home. Another roadblock.

After I left that job, I set up interviews with local landscaping companies. One day, while having lunch with my grandmother, I got a call asking if I could come in for an interview. I finished my meal, drove to the interview, and was offered the job on the spot. I started the next day. I actually enjoyed this job before the unthinkable happened. To this day, I don't know if anyone—especially the owner—knows what happened that weekend, but that's okay. Karma will take care of it.

I took a few weeks off after leaving that job. People told me, "You need to stop staying at a job for only one to three years and then moving on." I wanted stability, but I wasn't going to risk my mental health for a paycheck. I had worked too hard to stay somewhere I was treated poorly. I understood the nature of the industry, but like anyone—man or woman—I just wanted respect.

I applied to jobs in my area, and a former coworker recommended me to an owner who wanted to hire me immediately. I met with him, stated my worth, and stood my ground. A few days later, I was told to report to work. I was warned, "You're going to have more rules because you're a girl." Red flag. But I was in charge of my department and didn't report to anyone except for paperwork. I stayed at this company for eight years and dealt with a lot—good and bad.

In 2019, I got pregnant. I expected support from my employer after years of dedication. Instead, I was told, "Great, now I have to hire someone with experience to replace you." When I said I planned on returning, I was told, "You don't get maternity leave; this isn't a field women typically work in." Even during COVID, I was expected to work up until I physically couldn't. I stopped working in early July, using my vacation days. I requested to work from home near my hospital, but was told to just "go to a different hospital" if I went into labor.

Reflecting on this, I think of a quote: "Don't put too much into a company that would have your job posted online hours after you die." I now know that's exactly what this company would do.

The day I had my daughter, I never got a congratulations from my boss, but I did get a "So when do you think you will be coming back to work?" I didn't even answer. I could see this company was no longer worth my time or effort, and I needed to leave.

When I got home, I took two months and spent every waking moment with my daughter. I was surviving off my vacation time, but I was doing alright and felt comfortable doing that. I wanted to take in all the time I could with her before returning to the workforce. After about two months, I was running out of money and knew I needed to get back to work. I wasn't ready for full-time work, so I looked into work-from-home jobs and started selling Scentsy. I made enough to survive, but I needed more.

I asked trusted friends and family who could watch my daughter two or three days a week so I could work, and I found someone. I started working part-time at a landscaping company where my now-husband worked. It was an alright company, though I knew its reputation, so my expectations were low. However, I knew I could make good money there, so I did it.

Things went well for a while. I made it clear that I had no interest in working during the winter, and they seemed fine with it—so they said. About three weeks into the winter, I got a call saying they had lost an operator for a skid steer and asked if I would be interested. They assured me the pay would be worth it since winter work wasn't in my contract. Needless to say, my parents and friends were rockstars, stepping in to care for my daughter. I am forever grateful because I made a lot of money that winter, which helped my daughter and me tremendously.

Everything was going smoothly. I had a decent truck for plowing, and I was put in charge of a "zone," meaning I oversaw three or four properties and the crews working on them. The owner had me meet with a guy who ran the construction department to go over the properties before the snow started. As soon as I got into the truck with him, he said, "I know you." I looked at him and asked, "How?" He said, "I've been following you in this field for a long time. You used to pick up product at _____ in Woburn, right?" I confirmed and asked how he knew that. He told me he worked there. That's when I realized who he was.

I remembered him from the distributor. Back in my early 20s, the owner of that distributor had warned me to stay away from him, calling him a predator. He looked different now, but as soon as I put two and two together, I felt nervous being alone in the truck with him.

After that ride, I avoided him like the plague. He started doing things that made me uncomfortable—putting his arm around me, grabbing my waist, pulling me closer. One day in the office, he blocked the hallway, leaned in, and said, "So, where's my kiss?" I don't like being backed into a corner, so I grabbed him by the jacket, pushed him against the door, and said, "Talk to me again, and I will stab you." Then I walked away.

He wouldn't quit. It was bringing me back to past trauma. I had heard things about him, but I didn't know what he was capable of. Would he take things further, or was he all talk?

During snowstorms, he sent inappropriate text messages, asking for "spicy pictures" to get him through the storm. I ignored them. He then complained to the owner that I wasn't responding. The owner told me I needed to start answering him or face suspension. I felt sick. The next time I saw him, I told him, "If you're so upset about me not answering, maybe you should show the owner the messages you've been sending me and let him see why." Naturally, he had nothing to say and walked away.

The final straw came when I was in the shop getting ready for a storm. As I pulled on my rain gear over my cargo pants, I heard him say, "Looks good from this side." I ignored him, but the second I finished, he grabbed my waist. I spun around and swung at him. Then I got in my truck, spun my tires, and drove off. I texted the owner, saying we needed to talk after the storm. He agreed.

The next morning, I texted my boss, asking where he was. He said he was heading to the yard. I asked who else would be there, and when he mentioned the man I needed to complain about, I suggested meeting at Dunkin' Donuts instead. He asked if everything was okay. I said, "No."

At Dunkin', I told him everything, showed him the texts, and urged him to check the security cameras. He apologized and said he would look into it. A few days later, he called me into the office to meet with HR. When I arrived, the man was nowhere in sight—the owner had told him not to come in.

HR asked me a million questions. After an hour, I was told they would be in touch. Three days later, the owner called. The man was on paid suspension while HR investigated. They interviewed eleven employees, all of whom confirmed his behavior—towards me, other female employees, even male coworkers and clients. His work phone contained inappropriate pictures from female employees and clients. HR apologized, saying no one should have to endure that at work. They promised a decision soon.

Eleven days later, I was called back in. When I arrived, several coworkers were in the lobby, all told to come in. I had no idea things would spiral like this. I had simply wanted him in a different department. The owner had assured me there was an open-door policy, that I would always be heard.

I was called in first. A folder sat at the end of the table. The owner was at the other end, with two HR reps on either side. "What's going on?" I asked.

"Open the folder," the owner said.

I read it three or four times. My heart dropped. The owner looked me in the eye and said, "_____ makes me a lot of money. I don't like that you've created waves in my company. Effective immediately, you are no longer employed here."

I stared at him in disbelief. "Are you kidding me?" I looked at the HR reps—they lowered their heads. I turned back to the owner. "This is why people don't speak up. I hope nothing ever happens to your daughters because clearly, you will never defend them." Then I walked out.

Outside, my coworkers asked what happened. "I'm fired," I said and walked to my car. I was shaking, angry, sad—a million emotions at once. I didn't know what to do. But I had to go home to my daughter, the light of my life. She couldn't see me this upset. I needed to pick myself up and find another job—fast.

After calming down, I picked up my daughter and went home. I held her, reminding myself that I had to keep going. A few days later, I reached out to a friend who owned a trucking and utility company. He offered me a job immediately.

It was a great job. I made a lot of money and, as a bonus, worked with my brother, which made me feel even safer. I stayed there for almost a year. Nothing bad happened, but my stomach issues flared up, and the physical labor became too much.

That same month, I took a leap of faith—I started my own business. My husband and his son worked full-time for our company, and I worked in the city. We made great money and loved running a family-operated business.

I once found a quote from an anonymous survivor: "Although I wish I recognized what abuse was earlier, being able to talk to someone openly about what happened is the biggest gift in the world, and it makes me realize it's not my fault." I now understand that more than ever.

Chapter 7

"Why Do You _____ Like That?"

"You are the author of your own life. Write it boldly, write it fearlessly, and write it well enough that people will want to read every chapter."

I am one of those people who will tell you how it is. I really wanted to make a chapter about this because I was not your typical girl growing up. I got a lot of crap from people saying exactly what the chapter title says: "Why do you DRESS like that?" "Why do you TALK like that?" "Why do you ACT like that?" This will be the shortest chapter in my book, but I felt it was necessary to add something like this in.

When I was younger, as I said before, I was just your typical "tomboy." I played on the Police League Football Team for my town. I wore baggy clothes because that was what I was comfortable in. Ever since I was little, I was made fun of for wearing those clothes, wearing band shirts, and always wearing hoodies. I was called "gay." I was called a "slob" and everything in between. I was never really into fashion; I always just wore what was comfortable for me. Even for prom or any fancy outing, I would dress nicely, but I refused to spend money on clothes. I never felt the need to spend money on clothes—until I got sober.

When I got sober, I felt like I needed a whole new identity, and I had all this extra money to burn. I went out and bought an entirely new wardrobe—close to $1,000 worth of clothes and shoes—80% of which I didn't even wear. I still have some of it in my closet now, almost seven years later, with tags still on, shoes with the paper still inside, and jackets that have been on specialized hangers so long that the shoulders are permanently puffed up.

Getting sober was a great time in my life, but it was difficult because I needed to find a different fix. For me, that was clothing and soda. Even after spending so much money on all these fancy new clothes, it never actually made me feel better (big surprise). All it did was break me financially, just like alcohol and pills had. Now that I have been sober for a while, I know I need my outlets. I am still guilty of drinking way too much soda when I'm stressed, but I would rather drink soda than alcohol, which would lead me back to pills. I am comfortable with who I am now. I am a hoodie kind of girl, and I love it.

The first time someone asked me, "Why do you talk like that?" I was confused. I remember it was back in middle school. I used to talk goofy. I laughed a lot, joked with people—don't get me wrong, I could have a serious conversation when needed, but there was always something funny coming out of my mouth. I kept a smile on a lot of people's faces, even when I couldn't keep a smile on my own.

When someone asked me, "Why do you talk like that?" what should have come out of my mouth was, "Because I like to be happy. Leave me alone." But instead, I changed how I talked at school. I started talking like the girls who made fun of me. I talked about boys even though I had no interest in anyone. I calmed down how I spoke to people to the point that a teacher asked me what was wrong and if something was going on. That was how much I allowed someone to control me.

As I got older, I cared a lot less about what people thought of how I talked, which led me to drafting this book. I wanted to talk about the things that are hard to talk about. Any of my friends can tell you—I'm that friend who will tell you how it is. I won't sugarcoat things. I'll tell you if you're wrong, help you figure out a solution, but I will tell you when you are wrong.

Asking me, "Why do you act like that?" warrants a long-winded answer. I act like "that" because that's who I am. And don't get me wrong, I also changed how I acted to fit what was cool or expected for a long time. It took me a long time to find myself and just be comfortable with who I was. I felt like I needed to be a certain way around certain people, like I had to water myself down for people to like me.

Growing up, I remember thinking I needed to act a certain way around some of my mom's side of the family, but I could be my true, crazy, funny self with my dad's side. I knew how to put a mask on when needed so I could fit in wherever I had to. That doesn't mean I had to change who I was (for the most part), but there were certain topics I could and couldn't talk about.

As I got older, I stopped caring what people thought of my opinions. I said how I felt, and people could take it or leave it. I have friends who share my views, and I have friends who don't. I have two best friends—two women who have been by my side through everything. They have been the biggest people in my children's lives, and they are two of the best women in this world. Here's the catch: One of my best friends and I vote exactly the same. The other? We vote very differently. But I'm still best friends with both of them, and I wouldn't change a thing.

Here's your chapter-mandated "Glamor Word Picture" update: I am lying on the floor, surrounded by a bunch of my daughter's stuffed animals because, as she put it, "They are helping you write your book, Mommy." Well, okay then. At least I'm in work clothes while doing this. My daughter is sitting at her Baby Shark desk, watching Miss Rachel. I have never been so ready for bed in my life.

Stay exactly who you are supposed to be, and don't let people change how you dress, how you talk, or how you act. I watered myself down for so many years. I stopped myself from speaking my mind, speaking up for myself, and advocating for myself.

Chapter 8

Finding Yourself

"You need to find yourself first; then everything else will follow behind."

This quote by Charles De Lint has always stuck with me. For those who don't know, he's a brilliant author who writes fantasy fiction. I love this quote because finding myself was something I really struggled with—especially doing it in the order he described. Find yourself first, then everything will fall into place. I struggled with this, and sometimes I still do. To this day, I tend to take on too much before finishing one thing, which drives me nuts. At 35, I finally felt like I had figured myself out and was happy with who I had become. But every time I thought I had things figured out, something else happened, forcing me to learn something new, to handle things I had never dealt with before. At this point, though, I don't think there's much more I need to adapt to—at least, I hope not.

I've struggled with finding myself since I was little. Growing up, I saw different sides of my family and how my parents talked about them. I'd hear, "Don't be like this aunt, but be like this uncle." I felt like I was being pulled in a million directions—talk this way, act that way, have this kind of job. I assumed that "being myself" meant being what everyone expected me to be. My life goal became trying to be exactly who my parents wanted me to be. The problem was, my parents had vastly different ideas about who that was.

My mom wanted me to have a high-paying office job, specifically as a landscape designer or architect. I did get my certification, but I didn't use it much. Even when I had my construction company, I barely used it. The truth is, in my 20+ years in the green industry and construction field, I can count on both hands how many times a client asked for a hand-drawn design. Over the last decade or so, people want 3D renderings from a computer program. I enjoy hand-drawn design—it takes skill. You need to understand plants, spacing, height, everything. But the program I used when I was in business required no skill at all. Any homeowner could spend $150 on a program and design their own yard. It was disappointing. You'd just scroll through a database of plants, pick one, and the program would tell you everything—its height, spread, colors. It made the process almost mindless.

Another challenge in finding myself was my parents' very different approaches to speaking one's mind. My mom was more about keeping things to yourself if there was a chance someone wouldn't like what you said. My dad, on the other hand, encouraged me to speak my mind. He loved that I worked in the field as an operator. With him, I didn't have to be "proper." I could be more open about my views and felt more comfortable with his side of the family.

Both of my parents empowered me in different ways. My mom encouraged me socially—she always told me to have fun, live my best life, and treat people right because good karma would come back. My dad empowered me professionally. He taught me to stand up for myself and, as people say today, "match energies." As I got older, I took a little from both and became my own person. It took me a long time to balance what my parents taught me while still having my own values and identity.

I've had two major moments in my life where I struggled with finding myself. The first was when I got sober. The second was at the end of 2024, at 36, when I decided to switch careers after being in the green industry and construction field since I was 13. Let's talk about what that looked like for me.

By the way—eight chapters in, and I'm still uncomfortable writing about myself. But I'm getting there, slowly but surely.

When I got sober in December 2017, I struggled—not just with sobriety, but with figuring out who I was after getting sober. I quickly learned that not everyone was my friend. Want to find out who your true friends are? Get sober. It's eye-opening.

One moment still sticks with me. Back when I was married, I asked my best friend if her daughter would be my flower girl. She said no. I was mad for a while, but she told me it was because I wasn't present in her daughter's life. In my drinking and pill-popping haze, I didn't understand. But once I got sober, I realized she was absolutely right. To this day, it hurts that I missed out on that time with my niece—time I can never get back. But now that my mind is clear, I can be present. I can be the aunt I should have been and a better best friend.

Since high school, I was known as the party girl. I was at most parties, drinking, making everyone laugh, and doing stupid things I should have been afraid to do. I wasn't a "one-night stand" kind of girl—it wasn't me. I was flirtatious, I led guys on, but I rarely acted on anything. I just wanted to have fun.

Once I turned 21, I started bartending and made even more "friends." By "friends," I mean people who knew I could get them into the bar without paying a cover. Out of seven days a week, I was partying four to six nights. That was my identity. If you were bored and wanted to go out, everyone knew to call me. I was always ready, no matter the hour. I knew every bar and club within a 20-mile radius. I knew a lot of bands and had their schedules. I also had a truck and a license, so even though I should have been the designated driver—and even though I said I would be—I was often the person putting myself and others in danger by driving drunk.

When I got sober, I suddenly had all this spare time, extra money, and a failing marriage. Who the hell was I? The hardest part of sobriety wasn't quitting drinking—it was sitting with my feelings. That was rough. No matter what my mood, no matter what I was going through, a few drinks and some pills had always "fixed" it.

I didn't know what to do with myself. At first, I binge-watched Netflix, but I can only sit still for so long. Then I started shopping—spending money like crazy. That worked for a few months until I was broke and out of closet space.

Then I tried reading, but again, I can't sit still for too long. I just didn't know who I was anymore.

I tried calling my old drinking friends, but once they realized I was sober, they stopped answering. I started getting depressed. I threw myself into work just to stay busy. If I was working, I wasn't thinking. I wasn't stuck in my own head. I went to AA meetings. I spent time with the few friends I had left. I just did everything I could to avoid being alone with my thoughts.

Now, for this chapter's glamorous word picture:

I'm sitting on the couch, drinking Crystal Light out of a cute little wine glass I bought at my daughter's school craft fair. I'm wrapped in a Bluey blanket, writing this while half-listening to the news about the inauguration tomorrow. As always—very glam, very demure, and very much *not* what the editors imagined when they first talked to me.

Moving forward, I struggled with figuring out who I was while still trying to be the person my parents wanted me to be. I was slowly learning more about myself, becoming happier with the new me. I was finding better ways to handle my emotions and discovering the outlets I needed to stay grounded. It felt like I went from the truck-driving party girl to the truck-driving homebody overnight. Looking back, I'm completely okay with that—it's what kept me alive.

For a long time, I felt like I was finally thriving. I had survived assault, sobriety, divorce, brutal fights with my parents, and so much more. Then, in July 2020, I had my daughter, and my world became bright and beautiful again. My life felt like it was back on track. I was enjoying every second of motherhood, preparing to return to work, and continuing my education in Counterterrorism—not that I had any real plans to change careers. I was still landscaping and enjoying it. But life had other plans.

In 2021, I opened my business, North Shore Enhancement—a full-service landscaping and construction company on the North Shore of Massachusetts. I loved owning my own business. I had built a strong reputation since 2003, and despite all the struggles, I had fought my way through. I was featured in national magazines, gave talks across the country, mentored many people, and had companies competing to hire me. I never received a bad review, and every job I got was through word of mouth. When I launched North Shore Enhancement, many of my previous clients followed me, which speaks volumes about my reputation in the field.

The biggest challenge I faced was opening during COVID. You wouldn't think it mattered much, but I had never encountered such entitled, angry people in my entire career. With everyone stuck at home, they turned to "YouTube University" and "TikTok Tech," suddenly believing they were experts in landscaping. For the first time, I had clients hiring a professional while insisting they knew how to do the job better. Some of my favorite lines included:

- "I know my plants are dead now, but I saw how to do it on YouTube, so there must be something wrong with the plant."

- "I saw it on TikTok, so I know I did it right."

- "My husband helped his grandfather build a patio when he was six, so he knows what he's doing—I don't understand why the patio sank."

- And my personal favorite: "I saw a guy on TikTok from California do it this way," as if California's climate, soil, and plants were the same as Boston's.

There was no reasoning with people. Between TikTok and YouTube, they knew everything. That said, 98% of my clients were incredible. I made mistakes in my business, but I always made things right, whether with clients or distributors.

For example, one client made a down payment, but due to miscommunication about scheduling, the job wasn't completed in time for their graduation party. I still did the work but gave them a generous discount and a free hour of weeding from one of my enhancement crews.

Another instance still sticks with me. A longtime client, a wonderful older gentleman, had put down a deposit for a patio installation. A month before the project was set to begin, he passed away. His daughter called, letting me know they needed time to figure things out. I assured her there was no rush and immediately got a bank check to refund the deposit.

A few weeks later, she asked to meet. When I handed her the check, she surprised me by pushing it back. She told me her father trusted me, loved my company, and considered me family. Over the years, I had done little things for him—bringing in groceries, changing lightbulbs, even painting a few rooms—and never accepted a tip. She asked me to keep the deposit and build the patio at her home instead.

I thought about it, then remembered what my father had taught me: "Keep humility, whether at work or in life, and you'll always be able to sleep at night with a clear conscience." I took the check back and slid her father's contract across the table.

"This is your price," I told her.

She looked at me, confused. "But this is my father's contract. There's no way it's the same price."

I explained how much her father meant to me and my crew, how he always welcomed us with open arms (sometimes literally, ha!). She agreed, and a month later, we installed the patio. I also surprised her with a memorial plaque bearing her father's name, placed next to a new birdbath in the mulch bed—he had loved watching the birds every morning.

These are the kinds of jobs that made me love what I did.

One last story—shorter, I promise.

An elderly woman called on a weekend, needing her yard cleaned up. She had lost her husband five years earlier and could no longer maintain it herself. She didn't want anything fancy—just enough space to plant flowers in his memory each spring.

Her budget was far too low for what the job required. I told her I'd come up with a plan and call her back. The next day, I let her know we'd do the work for her, but instead of money, I asked her to bake the same cookies she had me try when we first met.

She agreed.

On the day of the job, I had her stay inside with the blinds closed so she couldn't see the yard until we were done. When she finally stepped outside, I helped her to the deck. She opened her eyes and immediately started crying. She hugged me tighter than anyone ever has.

As she took it all in, I led her down the steps. Under the layers of leaves, she rediscovered a small patio she hadn't seen since her husband passed. A memorial stone for their late dog was now visible again.

Through her tears, she said, "I can't believe this. No amount of money or cookies will ever be enough of a thank you."

That job will always stay with me.

There was no real "breaking point" for me. I had just been thinking more about what I went to school for, especially after starting to draft my book. Writing this book has been the most therapeutic thing I've done in a long time, helping me work through a lot of my issues. When I seriously started considering a career change, I found myself struggling with the same insecurities I had when I got sober—who am I if I'm not doing landscaping, running equipment, or driving trucks? I went back and forth on it for months, but by late November 2024, I decided it was time to do what I truly wanted. I'm still the same me—I just have a different career path now.

I'm incredibly grateful for my husband's support. And as a bonus, when we closed North Shore Enhancement, he opened his own business to continue doing what he loves: stonework. I'm so proud of him, just like he's proud of me. After so many years, I finally feel like I've found myself. I'm comfortable with who I am, and I've found my people.

The last thing I want to talk about is something that happened more recently. It might sound stupid to some, but I want to put it out there for anyone who felt the same way. When I was landscaping and doing construction, if I hit a roadblock, I could fix things in minutes. I knew everyone, I knew different angles to approach problems, and I could recover from anything pretty easily.

Then, in January 2025, TikTok was banned. Granted, it only lasted 16 hours, but it still shook me a bit. Over four or five months, I had built a following of over 1,200 people—people who commented on my posts about my book, attended my live streams, and even asked about pre-orders. I used other social media platforms to promote my book, but none were as successful as TikTok. That was where I made my name and got my book noticed.

I know some people might think, "1,200 followers isn't that many," but to me, it was huge. I never tried to make a name for myself on social media, so knowing that 1,200 people took time out of their day to engage with my content was humbling—and honestly, really cool to watch.

When TikTok went down, I panicked. How was I going to advertise my book? How would I do live streams to interact with readers? I downloaded a few other apps to try and build a following, but I didn't understand them the way I understood TikTok. I feel ridiculous even writing about it, but that short time made me really nervous. In landscaping and construction, I could always find a way to fix things, but this was different.

I know how stupid it sounds—getting anxious over an app—but, like millions of other small businesses and authors, TikTok helped with exposure and income. It wasn't just an app for funny videos. It changed lives. So many small-town singers made it big because of TikTok. So many small authors, like myself, found a community of like-minded people who supported each other and helped each other grow an audience. The thought of losing that scared all of us.

At the end of the day, I'm proud of myself for finding my way and becoming the person I am today. I've been through a lot, but I came out on top. And if you're reading this, I want you to know that you can find yourself too.

Chapter 9

Becoming A "Bonus Parent"

"Biology is the least of what makes someone a mother." This quote by Oprah Winfrey resonates deeply with me. Becoming a "bonus mom" has been one of the most rewarding, crazy, and emotional rides of my life.

When I first met my now-husband, he told me he had an adult son. I assured him that was fine. I've always believed that when you love someone with children, you love and protect those children as if they were your own. From the day I met my stepson, I did just that. I loved him, supported him, and tried to make his life a little easier after all he had been through.

We had a strong relationship from the start. He was struggling with sobriety, and since I was already sober, we connected on that level. We talked about his past trauma, and I offered solid advice to help him move forward. I introduced him to my AA group, where he quickly made friends. He was doing well—until he wasn't. My husband and I stood by him through every challenge, making sure he had what he needed to succeed.

As time went on, stress weighed heavily on him. I tried to be the person I needed when I first got sober, but I realized I was doing too much. Every time he had an episode or a slip-up, I was the first person he called. He reminded me so much of myself during my early sobriety struggles, and I made the mistake of being the support I had once needed rather than the support he needed.

In the fall of 2022, my stepson asked me something I never expected: "Will you adopt me?" He told me I had been more of a mother to him than his biological mother ever was. He wanted to sever the last tie to her, allowing him to fully heal. I didn't hesitate, but I did ask if it was possible since he was an adult and if he had discussed it with his dad. He had done his research and found that Massachusetts allows adult adoptions. His therapist agreed that it would help his mental health, so we started the process.

We gathered paperwork and submitted it to the courthouse, but we were missing a few forms. By then, landscaping season had begun, and things got put on hold.

Then, in May 2023, my stepson had the worst relapse of his sobriety journey, requiring a lengthy hospital stay. While he was there, we worked on our relationship as a family. I was proud of him for opening up and getting the help he needed. But while he was healing, the people he once trusted were destroying his home, squatting in his place, and using it as a party spot. When he was released, we spent days cleaning and reorganizing his living space.

He was doing well—until he wasn't. He realized the people he once called friends were toxic. They harassed him, showed up at his place uninvited, and even robbed him. He kept it from us at first, not wanting us to think he was falling back in with them.

By the fall of 2023, the stress overwhelmed him. In December, my husband and I were blindsided when he disappeared, heading north without telling us. At first, he stayed in contact, but then—radio silence. He had mentioned being in southern Maine, so when we lost contact, I pinged his phone and contacted the authorities. They found him in the woods and assured us he was okay, saying he would call us soon. He never did.

Panic set in. We called the police daily, drove to Maine to search, posted on social media, and reached out to his friends. No one had heard from him. A week later, I filed a missing person's report. The officer dismissed my concerns, saying, "He's an adult; he won't be at the top of anyone's list." That didn't sit right with me, but I kept pushing. I reached out to Missing People of America, who took updated pictures and spread the word nationwide.

Months passed. We continued searching, making calls, and checking social media. Then, nearly a year later—just weeks before the anniversary of his disappearance—we got a lead. A woman called, saying she knew where he was. She gave me an address and a phone number.

I ran to my husband, tears streaming down my face. "We found him!" We texted my stepson that night, but he didn't respond. Two days later, my phone buzzed—it was him. Relief flooded me. We set up a visit, and when we finally saw him, there were tears, questions, and overwhelming gratitude.

Being a "bonus mom" has been an emotional journey, but it has only made our family stronger. Watching my husband and his son rebuild their bond has been heartwarming. Blood doesn't define family—love, understanding, and resilience do.

Chapter 10

Losing a Loved One

"Those we love don't go away; they walk beside us every day. Unseen, unheard, but always near. Still loved, still missed, and very dear."

Losing someone is never easy, whether it is family or a friend. It feels like a piece of your heart has broken away forever. Everyone believes different things about death, and as much as I didn't want to touch on religion—screw it, I'm going to. Each religion has its own beliefs when it comes to death.

I'll start with mine to break the ice. I follow a Native/Pagan-based belief. I believe that when someone passes, their body is gone, but their spirit remains. The spirits of those who have passed move on and journey to places they knew on Earth.

Christians believe that, as long as you follow the word of the Lord, your soul will be welcomed into Heaven, where you will meet God and remain for eternity. On the flip side, Christians believe that if you have not lived by the word of the Lord, your soul will remain in Hell and be punished for eternity.

Judaism also believes in Heaven and Hell, but depending on who you talk to, some believe you are judged the day you die, while others believe you will be judged by God and the Messiah on the Day of Judgment, Rosh Hashanah, based on your actions from the past year.

Hinduism teaches that when a person passes, they are reborn into another physical being to live another life. This belief is heavily tied to karma. If you are a good person in this life, you will be rewarded in the next, but if you have not been good, you will likely suffer in your next life.

I'm not going to go through every religion, but I wanted to touch on the ones my friends and family are a part of. I could have Googled it, but we don't believe everything we read on the internet...right? The final religion I'll mention is Islam. In Islam, when a person passes away, they await Judgment Day. Two angels question the soul about their life choices. If they answer correctly, they go to Barzakh, a place of waiting. If they answer improperly, their souls are tortured by angels for eternity.

So why did I bring up religion? Because everyone finds peace in death in different ways. Some beliefs are more extreme than others, and some seem very peaceful. One of the biggest things I have noticed over the years when it comes to death is how selfish people can become. They tend to want to do things their way instead of honoring how the deceased wanted to be celebrated. If someone spent time writing a will to express their final wishes, just follow it.

Now let's talk about the hard part. Everyone has faced this: the financial burden of death. Funerals are expensive, and I believe the "Death Industry" (if that's not what it's called, I'm rolling with it) is one of the most stressful industries around. Families are already grieving, and then they get hit with a massive bill.

In 2024, a friend of mine lost her mother to cancer. She was next of kin and had to make all the calls. When she called the funeral home, they told her it would cost $1,300 just to come and get her mother's body. She didn't have the money upfront and asked about a payment plan. They refused, saying they couldn't retrieve the body until the bill was paid in full. That blew my mind. I know not all funeral homes are like that, but shame on those that are. I ended up lending her the amount she was short, but the fact that these places can be so heartless makes me sad.

I remember the first time I experienced loss. It was my Nana, and she passed away in 2000 when I was in middle school. I was very close to her; she even lived with us for a while. We did so much together. I remember watching wrestling with her and my brothers in the living room—she would cheer right along with us. Every time she got sick and needed an ambulance, she always refused to go until we told her that handsome firemen would come to get her. Then she was all for it. Losing her at around eleven years old was tough. The hardest part was knowing that sometimes my bad attitude spilled onto her, and I regret that now. But there were so many good times, too. My favorite memory? On her 90th birthday, all she wanted was to ride on the back of my dad's Harley. The pictures from that day were epic. I will always miss her—she was strong, resilient, and had no filter, which I loved about her.

In 2008, I lost my great-grandparents in Idaho. My great-grandmother was the one I mentioned earlier in my book, the one who used to walk laps around her garage for exercise. They were the sweetest people, always donating time to their church. They were the perfect example of what a marriage should be. They were married for 73 years (just a month shy of 74) when they passed away, only three days apart, at 93 and 91 years old. They married young, at 18 and 20. My great-grandparents taught me so much, and my dad's stories about his grandfather were amazing. One memory stands out: I was about ten, visiting Idaho for a family reunion. I had a terrible epilepsy headache, the kind that made it impossible to move, see, or speak. My great-grandfather knelt next to the couch, took my hand, and asked if he could say a blessing. I couldn't respond, but he did it anyway. As he rested his head on mine, I felt an odd sense of calm. Though his lips weren't moving, I could hear words in my head. I fell asleep and woke up hours later, completely fine. Normally, when I fall asleep with a headache, I wake up feeling worse. That day was different.

In 2014, I lost my grandmother—my mother's mom. She played a huge role in my life. I spent so much time at her house growing up. She was so cool. Her house had two extra bedrooms, one that used to be my mom's when she was little and another that belonged to my uncles. My cousins and I took turns sleeping in the "Princess" room, my mom's old room. It was always the fun house. We had Big Wheels in the backyard, a garden where we learned to plant crops, and a safe place to play. Like my Nana, my grandmother had no filter and loved her family deeply.

2015 changed my life forever. I lost two major people within a week. First, my grandfather—the Marine I mentioned earlier. He meant everything to me. We had a camper in Kennebunk, Maine, and he had one right next to ours. We spent nearly every weekend there, fishing, playing basketball, and mini-golfing. When my grandmother went into a nursing home, he no longer wanted the camper. I helped him get it ready to sell. We often took long drives together, and I always laughed at how bad other drivers were—not him, though. I called him "Tampa" because when I was little, every word started with a T. Instead of Grandpa, he was Tampa. I hope I made him proud by trying to join the Marines and everything I'm doing now.

The second person I lost that year was my brother. He was my inspiration for everything, and he still is. He had Muscular Dystrophy and passed at 38, but damn, did he leave a legacy. He holds a Guinness World Record, and as far as I know, no one has beaten it—probably because no one else is crazy enough to try. He was my brother, my shoulder to cry on, my best friend. He always knew his life would be short, but he had an amazing attitude. Growing up with epilepsy, I tried to live like he did—in the moment. He passed away the day of Tampa's funeral. Not a day goes by that I don't think about him.

Why did I share these stories? To remind everyone that we all make mistakes. My great-grandmother once told me, "Never go to bed angry." If your last conversation with someone wasn't good, make it right. Tomorrow isn't promised. Cherish every moment. And always keep the memories alive.

Chapter 11

Raising A Strong Girl

To My Beautiful Daughter, Kenna,

You are my world. I love you with all my heart and soul. You have given me a purpose in life again—a reason to live. Your smile and laughter bring me endless joy. I love spending time with you and all the silly things we do together. You inspire me more than you will ever know. You are creative, caring, and so strong—both physically and mentally. I am beyond proud of everything you do, and I promise to make sure no one ever puts out your flame.

No matter where this crazy life takes you, know you always have a place at Mom's if you need it. You are loved and admired more than words can express. You are an incredible daughter, and you continue to amaze me every day. One day, you will have to stand your ground without me there, but whatever you do, know that I will always be in your corner. I have seen the bad in this world, but I have also seen so much good. See the brightness every day, and always know your worth.

Love Always,

Your Mom <3

I gave birth to my daughter in July 2020, and since then, she has been my reason to live. As I draft this book, she is four years old—smart, kind, and full of love. I know I am raising a strong little girl, and strong little girls grow into confident women. I want her to know that having feelings is okay, but acting on them without thought, as I often did growing up, is not. I want her to reach out and help others but never allow herself to be taken advantage of.

As I wrote in my letter, one day, she will have to stand her ground without me. As much as I love my husband and as much as I ignored my father's advice, I am teaching her to never rely on a man—to always be able to take care of herself. This world will throw storms her way, and I want her to know how to weather them. I know she will shatter glass ceilings one day, and I cannot wait to see what she does with her life.

When I was growing up, I never planned on having children. My sole focus was the Marines and work—no exceptions. But life happens, and I was blessed with a best friend. I truly believe that raising a little girl takes a village. As I mentioned earlier in this book, women are losing their voices, dumbing themselves down, and not giving themselves enough credit. I was so happy to have a daughter because my two best friends—two of the bravest, strongest women I know—are her godmothers. They have always looked out for her. The three of us are all girl moms, and I love it.

I know this chapter is short, but my daughter is everything. I wanted to include something in this book that she can always come back to when she needs it.

And for those of you who have daughters, too… yeah, I'm broke. But I wouldn't change it for anything.

Chapter 12

Now As a Business Owner

"Success is the sum of small victories added together to make something great."

Growing up, I watched my dad run a successful business, and after everything I experienced working for others, it just felt right to start my own. I wanted to stop making money for other people and create a safe place for those who loved this field to work every day.

I officially opened my business in March 2021, and it felt like a dream come true. As I've said before, I tend to try doing everything at once, and in a short period of time. My husband had to reel me back in when I first opened—I wanted everything immediately. I didn't want to work out of the house; I wanted office space. I didn't want a used truck; I wanted a new one. We ended up working from home for the first five months, but then we found office space through a longtime friend in North Reading. That's when things really started to take off.

The office had everything I wanted—enough room for two desks, one for me and one for my office manager. We had yard space for our trucks, trailers, and stone. It felt like an early win for my company.

We stayed there until December 2022, when we outgrew the space and moved to a new office in Peabody, MA. This time, we had two offices—one for my husband and me, and another for my office manager. We settled in for a while, but then things took a turn. The building owner signed a deal with the state to allow undocumented migrants to live there. Suddenly, companies were dealing with theft. Clients visiting businesses in the building saw people sleeping in the hallways. The common area, which had once been a quiet space to eat lunch, became chaotic—food and drinks went missing from the shared fridge, and loud music played daily.

I filed two police reports after our things were stolen, but nothing changed. When I asked the building manager why, I was told the owner was receiving thousands of dollars a month from the state to house these individuals. The final straw came when my office manager saw a few people looking around my office while I had stepped out. She no longer felt safe.

When we first moved in, there were about 35 businesses in the building. By the time we left, only six remained.

In July 2024, I began searching for a new office space and found one—also in Peabody—not far from the old location. My office manager and I toured it together, and we both loved it. It was within budget, so I took it.

Remember when I mentioned my 1,100-square-foot office space, the one where I drafted my books but primarily ran the construction company? This was that place. And let me tell you, when I got this office, I felt on top of the world.

I had my own massive corner office. My office manager had a great space. We had a third office for our fleet mechanic, a conference room where my husband had his drafting table for stonework designs, and even a showroom for all the beautiful stone we sold and installed. I was at the top of my game—our clients were amazing, reviews were stellar, employees were happy, and we were making money. Life couldn't have been better.

In September 2024, my husband and I got married. The guys got ready for the wedding right at the office, giving my husband a chance to show off everything we had worked so hard for to out-of-state family members. We were on cloud nine.

Then, in October, everything came crashing down.

We were working on our biggest job to date in the northern part of the state. Seven days a week, for over a month, we poured everything into that project. The homeowners were thrilled, referring us to friends and family, texting me daily about how amazed they were. Then, suddenly, they changed their tune and demanded a full refund.

When I asked why, they wouldn't give me a straight answer. Our distributors had been inspecting the work throughout the project, confirming everything was flawless. The town building department had also approved it. We had even completed extra work beyond the contract. Yet, out of nowhere, they wanted their money back.

They hired a lawyer, claiming nothing had been installed correctly. When I asked the lawyer who had said that, he had no answer. I reminded him that both our distributors and the town had approved the work, and suddenly, he stopped responding.

I later spoke with the building inspector, who told me this happens all the time—people take out massive loans for home renovations, realize they're in over their heads, and then try to strong-arm contractors into refunds before the banks catch on.

I submitted all the necessary documents to fight back. But then, for the first time in my career, someone played *the card* against me.

They told the bank I refused to finish the job because they were part of the LGBTQ community and that I was *sexist*.

What?!

In the end, I won the case. But this was my breaking point.

I know what some people might be thinking: *"You're really going to give up 23 years in an industry you fought so hard to succeed in over one bad client?"*

The answer is both yes and no.

Yes, because in 23 years, I had *never* encountered anything like this. I had *never* needed a lawyer. After I refused to issue a refund, they and their friends launched an online smear campaign—posting false accusations about me all over community pages, the BBB, Yelp, and beyond. Most of these people didn't even live in my state.

Everything was in the contract they signed. No refunds for completed work. No refunds for custom-ordered materials. Yet I knew there was no coming back from this.

And no, because I had been considering a career change for years. I had always wanted to transition into the criminal justice field. This was my opportunity to make that change.

Before anyone gets the wrong idea—I have *zero* problems with the LGBTQ community. I fully support them. I am a minister, and every wedding I have officiated has been for LGBTQ couples. The issue wasn't their identity; it was the fact that instead of communicating like adults, they went straight to a lawyer, ignored my messages, and then played *the card* to try and manipulate the situation.

That's literally where the title of my book comes from.

Whatever card you're playing to get ahead—it's not the way to handle things. Don't play a card. Just talk. Whether you're a woman, a man, straight, gay, Black, white, brown—*whatever*—we are all human.

I judge people based on how they treat animals and other human beings, not who they love. But when people pull this kind of move, I lose all respect. I want to be respected for the work I do, *not* because I am a woman. I hope that makes sense.

Everyone is fighting a battle you may not see. Just be kind. Talk things out. Treat people with respect. It costs *zero* dollars to be a decent human being.

I have always been well-respected by my clients. I've gone above and beyond, even for the difficult ones. My bosses and colleagues haven't always treated me with respect, but seeing my clients happy made it all worthwhile.

2024 was the end of an era for me. And that's okay. Because in 2025, I'm onto bigger and better things.

To the clients who left amazing reviews, who took the time to chat with me, who paid on time, who referred me to friends and family—you are the *real* all-stars. You are the reason I never had to advertise. From March 2021 to December 2024, I never needed a single ad.

To the clients who sent me holiday cards—you brightened my days.

To the clients who supported me after my brother's passing in 2015, even before I owned my company, and to those who were amazing after I had my daughter—this was for all of you.

To my distributors—thank you for always having my back. Many of you encouraged me to go out on my own, and you gave me the confidence to do it. I hope I made you proud.

Chapter 13

Career Change in Your Thirties

"I love this quote because I feel it fits perfectly: "You miss 100% of the shots you do not take." Truer words have never been spoken by the legend, Mr. Wayne Gretzky.

Over the last two years, I had been talking more and more with my husband about making a career change, but I never had the guts to do it. My husband kept telling me how smart I am and how I should do this because if I don't do it now, I probably never will. Ladies, I know you understand—don't you hate it when they're right? So, for two years, we bounced around the idea of me making a career change. What happened at that job site was the straw that broke the camel's back for me. My stress level was through the roof, and for the first time in years, I felt backed into a corner with no way out.

In July of 2024, I began looking into what a career change would look like at my age. Not that I am old, but being in my mid-thirties, I would likely not be the first option for agencies—especially because it's not like I got into this field when I began schooling in 2011 at twenty-two years old. I figured I would have nowhere to go and would have to come crawling back to construction and landscaping, but I wanted to have my ducks in a row before making the official decision to leave behind what I had done for over two decades.

After looking into jobs, schooling, certifications, licensing, and so many other things, I sat down with my husband and told him, "I think I can do this. Like, I think this can really happen." I knew what direction I wanted to go in because I enjoyed doing interrogations and questioning in school, so I made the decision right then—I was going to be a Criminal Investigator.

In August of 2024, I began the licensing process to become an investigator, and I was actually doing really well in the classes. I figured I would finish my certification, lean on hopeful sales from my book, and look for a job then, but I received a text from a family friend saying, "When you get your license, I will have work for you right off the bat." So, I was looking down the barrel of a job with a criminal law firm! I could not believe what was happening—I hadn't even finished school yet, and I already had an offer. Never in a million years did I think this would be such a smooth transition.

I was so scared to make a career change at my age, but it is turning out better than I could have ever hoped. I was great at what I did for so many years. I enjoyed construction and landscaping, and it will always be a part of who I am. It is the career that both broke me and built me up. It is the career that darkened my soul but also lit up my life. It showed me just how evil and manipulative the world is, but it also showed me how loving people can be.

So, if you were to tell me you want to make a career change but aren't sure if you should, look at what needs to be done to reach your goals. It's never too late. I kick myself for thinking less of myself for so many years—to the point that I believed I was too stupid to do this.

now, seeing that I was able to get a job and be put right to work, I realize I should have followed my dreams fourteen years ago when I started schooling. I shouldn't have listened to the people I was with. I shouldn't have dumbed myself down. I shouldn't have doubted myself the way I did for so many years.

I know this chapter is called "Career Change in Your Thirties," but honestly, it doesn't matter how old you are. My dad is the perfect example. He had been doing flooring since he was a teenager and owned his own business before I was born. He closed the doors to his business in 2010 but still did flooring for a new company and longtime clients. I saw it was beating up his body—just like how construction was beating up mine. Then, in his sixties, my dad made a career switch from flooring to real estate investing. He still does flooring occasionally, especially in the houses he flips, but I am so incredibly proud of him for making the switch.

My mom is another perfect example of changing careers later in life. At around forty-eight years old, after being a stay-at-home mom from when I was born in 1988 until 2006, she went back to work. She started at a hospital near where she lived and is still there today. Everyone loves her—she's won awards and has even been the poster person for clean hands. She has done so much in her life, and I am so proud of her. Even though she went back to work when I was already in my senior year, she still made sure my brothers and I had everything we needed.

So, I skipped a few chapters in my "Glamor Word Picture" update. This book has been so therapeutic to write, and I am just taking in every moment while writing. But while I'm thinking about it—since we're nearing the end of the book—here we go. I am currently sitting at my desk in a Richard Simmons "Sweatin' to the Oldies" t-shirt, drinking some Crystal Light. I have been up since six o'clock writing, and I am exhausted, looking like a hot mess. Really pretty, I know.

My parents have inspired me in so many ways throughout my entire life. I have two brothers, but I was much younger than them. I am my mom's only child, but I was my dad's third. My brothers were nine and eleven years older than me, so, in a way, I kind of felt like an only child. I was usually hanging out alone or with my own friends because of the age difference. More than anything, when I decided to make this career change, I thought of my parents and how they made life-changing decisions later in life than I am now.

My mom inspired me because she had two stepsons, and she always loved and cared for them. Even after my parents divorced, she still showed up for my brothers when she needed to.

This career change is going to be a turning point in my life—not only because I'm becoming a criminal investigator, but also because I'm a writer! This is literally my first book, and I am so excited. Please, don't do what I did. Don't sell yourself short. Take the leap toward whatever it is you want to do because I promise you—it is worth it!

Katrina Eddy

Chapter 14

Marriage and Having a Partner

"You are my favorite place to be when I am searching for peace and love." I love this quote because, after all the dead-end relationships I have been in, my "place of peace" was found in substances—not in love or a relationship. It took a long time to break those walls down, but my husband kept telling me I was worth the wait. Our marriage is not perfect, but we are perfect for each other.

We met a decade or so before we started dating. I was in my early twenties, and we were at a trade show. We were in a class together and started chatting during one of the breaks. We really hit it off, but we were with other people at the time, so it remained a professional friendship. Over the years, we saw each other occasionally and enjoyed our conversations. He kept trying to get me to work with him, and the rest is history.

We have gone through a lot just in the last few years—likely more than most couples—but we have weathered it all together. We survived COVID, me losing my job after speaking up about sexual harassment, opening a business together, raising a daughter, closing the business, me becoming an author, my career switch, losses in our family, drama in our family, our wedding, health problems, and so much more.

I spent my entire life not knowing what a relationship was supposed to be like. I got so used to being emotionally, physically, financially, and mentally abused that I thought that's just how it was. I watched one of my brothers go through nothing but toxic relationships for years. Towards the end of my parents' marriage, it became toxic for them too, so I believed toxicity was just something that happened when you were with someone.

I'm not completely clueless—I know every relationship has problems, life happens—but in the past, I would just bow down to whatever my partner said. We were not a team. Now, I am a team with my husband.

One thing I hate is when I hear people say, "Oh, you need to ask your wife/girlfriend/boyfriend/husband if you can come out for a few beers after work? You're whipped/being controlled." First of all, I disagree wholeheartedly. That is not being whipped or controlled—that is being courteous to your significant other. You're letting them know your plans. In my past relationships, we just did our own thing, and that was that.

Find the person who sets your soul on fire and stay with them. Work through the speed bumps and just love each other through it all.

Chapter 15

Writing A Book

Holy shit, I wrote a book!

This chapter isn't going to be much—I just wanted to say thank you to everyone who took the time to follow the process over the last few months while I was writing. This has been an amazing ride, to say the least.

To everyone who helped me along the way and gave me advice, to my amazing publishing company for walking me through the process of my first book—thank you. To all my followers on TikTok and other social media platforms who asked questions, got on mailing lists for pre-orders, and ordered from the store—you are all amazing. My book would not be what it is without your support.

As strange as it sounds, thank you to the people who tried to put out my flame. You are the ones who, in turn, forced me to become the person I am today—the person I am now very proud of. The person who can look in the mirror and know her worth. The person who now knows what a relationship is supposed to be, whether with friends, family, or a significant other. The person who can now be a good role model for her daughter.

So, thank you. Thank you for putting me through hell. Thank you for showing me what rock bottom looks like, because now I am standing up. I am going to use the evil you forced onto me to help others who feel like they have nowhere to turn—just like I once did. And I promise you this: I am a strong woman. I have seen trauma firsthand, and I am ready to turn my trauma around.

If you are going through something in your life and need help finding a direction—or just want to vent—please email me directly. I promise I check every email and respond.

Katrina Eddy

Joshua Eddy – (Left)

Matthew Eddy - (Middle)

Katrina Eddy – (Right)

Made in United States
North Haven, CT
03 March 2025